Complete Library Skills

Grade 5

Published by Instructional Fair
an imprint of

 **Children's Publishing**

Author: Linda Turrell
Editor: Rebecca Warren

 Children's Publishing

Published by Instructional Fair
 An imprint of McGraw-Hill Children's Publishing
Copyright © 2004 McGraw-Hill Children's Publishing

Send all inquiries to:
McGraw-Hill Children's Publishing
3195 Wilson Drive NW
Grand Rapids, Michigan 49544

Complete Library Skills – grade 5
ISBN: 0-7424-1955-X

1 2 3 4 5 6 7 8 9 MAZ 09 08 07 06 05 04

Table of Contents

Introduction

By the time children reach fifth grade, they are ready and eager to use all the components of the library. They are capable of searching the shelves for fiction and nonfiction books; they enjoy discovering and examining reference materials; they are able to use computers both for searching and responding to what they have read.

Complete Library Skills—Grade Five is organized into three major sections: Where to Find It, What's Inside, and How to Use It. Terms in bold throughout the book can be found in the Glossary of Library Terms (see pages 122–123). This structure leads students through library activities from the earliest searches to the final report. Because computers are such an important part of library work, each section presents an excellent overview of using technology for everything from finding a book to creating a report. Look for this icon to find pages dealing with technology:

Where to Find It
In this section, students will practice performing searches, including activities on author, subject, title, and keyword search and evaluating Internet sites as sources. An overview of the Dewey Decimal Classification® and a thorough study of reference tools are also included. Students will develop dictionary skills and work with an almanac, atlas, and encyclopedia.

What's Inside
Once they have found a book, students need the skills to be able to determine if it will be useful. This section includes activities on the parts of a book—table of contents, index, glossary—and gives students practice using these elements to preview a book's content. By fifth grade, students will be using a variety of genres in their reading. Activities on the genres of literature will help familiarize them with the spectrum of books that are available and encourage them to expand their reading repertoire.

How to Use It
Once students have collected their materials, they need to know how to use them. For a fiction book, this may be obvious, but for a collection of nonfiction sources, it may require a bit more thought. This section gives students many resources to organize and make use of what they have read, including graphic organizers, note-taking, and citing sources.

A list of recommended titles for this age group appears on pages 118–119. Photocopy the Reading Log on page 120 for students to keep track of their reading throughout the year. Encourage students to read from a variety of genres. For those stellar achievers, the Library Superstar Award on page 121 provides positive reinforcement for great reading and research skills.

Name _____ Date _____

What's in the Library?

By the time you reach fifth grade, you've been in the library enough times to know the basics—a library is full of books. But do you know some of the other useful things that might be hiding someplace in your library?

▶ **Look at the list below. Draw a line to match each item to its correct description. Then choose two resources and write in how you might use each one.**

Resource	**Description**
1. atlas	**a.** disks with searchable databases or games
2. librarian	**b.** yearly publication with statistics on various events
3. shelf labels	**c.** spherical shaped map of the world
4. browser station	**d.** a book of words and their synonyms
5. information posters	**e.** a bound collection of maps
6. geographical dictionary	**f.** a professional who acts as your guide to the library
7. CD-ROMs	**g.** gives a range for what is located there
8. globe	**h.** collection of computers that search library catalog
9. almanac	**i.** colorful pictures with useful facts on them
10. thesaurus	**j.** lists spelling and facts about places in the world

▶ **How You Might Use Resources**

11. _____

_____

12. _____

_____

Analyzing a Research Question

➤ **Think of an area of interest that you would like to research. Answer the questions below to prepare for your information search. Write your answers on the lines provided.**

1. What topic would you like to research? _____

_____

_____

2. What research question could you use to locate

information for your topic? _____

_____

3. Analyze your question. Is it **general** or **specific**? If it's
general, rewrite the question to make it more specific.

_____

_____

_____

4. What are the **keywords** for your research question?

_____

_____

5. Can any of the keywords be combined to create

narrow search terms? Write them here. _____

_____

_____

Name _____ Date _____

The Card Catalog

The **card catalog** is a collection of author, title, and subject cards grouped together. It is a guide for you. Think of it as a giant telephone book for the books in the library. Each of the three types of cards gives the same information. The only item that is different is the first line of the card. The author card begins with the last name of the author. The title card begins with the title of the book, and the subject card begins with the subject of the book.

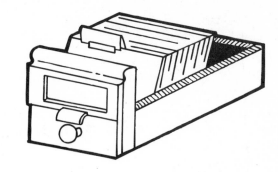

- If you know the title, choose the **title** section.
- If you know the author, choose the **author** section.
- If you know the subject but not title or author, choose the **subject** section.

▶ **Look at the situations below. Decide which section of the card catalog you would go to in order to find the answer. Write** *title*, *author*, **or** *subject* **on the line.**

1. _____ Your fifth-grade teacher has assigned the whole class a research project on leaves. Are there enough books in the library for all 25 of you?

2. _____ You want to look up *The Shady Tree* and find out who the author is.

3. _____ One of your favorite authors is Peter Leaf. You have read *The Shady Tree* and *Brett's Tree House*, but you want to find another book by the same author.

4. _____ Every fall, you wonder why leaves change color. How can you find a book to help you out?

Title Card

```
Fic        The Mystery of the Green Parrot
Fe

           Feather, Sally

           Mystery of the green parrot. Trenton, New Jersey.

           Pellet Press, 2003.

           63 p. illus.

           This is the story of a parrot and his adventures in his strange cage.

           1. Fiction—Parrot stories        I. Author
```

▶ **Use the title card above to answer the questions.**

1. What is the title of this book? _____

2. Who is the author? _____

3. Who is the publisher and where is the publisher located? _____

_____

4. What is the call number of this book? _____

5. Is this book fiction or nonfiction? _____

6. Are there pictures in this book? How do you know? _____

_____

Author Card

636.68   Pendleton, Polly
Pe

Caring for Your Pet Parrot. Austin: Texas.

Birdbrain Publications, 2003.

111 p. illus.

This book tells everything you need to know to care for a pet parrot in your home.

▶ **Use the author card above to answer the questions.**

1. What is the title of this book? _____

2. Who is the author? _____

3. Who is the publisher and where is the publisher located? _____

    _____

4. What is the call number of this book? _____

5. Is this book fiction or nonfiction? _____

6. Are there pictures in this book? How do you know? _____

    _____

Subject Card

636
Cr

PARROTS

Cracker, Stuart

The Well-Behaved Parrot. Los Angeles, California.

Pet Publications, 2003.

111 p. illus.

This book gives step-by-step instructions for managing the behavior of your pet parrot.

▶ **Use the subject card above to answer the questions.**

1. What is the title of this book? _____

2. Who is the author? _____

3. Who is the publisher and where is the publisher located? _____

   _____

4. What is the call number of this book? _____

5. Is this book fiction or nonfiction? _____

6. Are there pictures in this book? How do you know? _____

   _____

Name _____   Date _____

Media Card

Did you know that libraries are also sometimes called **media centers**? This is because the library contains much more than just books. Your school library may also contain cassette tapes, CDs, videos, posters, or other non-book resources. If you look at the card catalog, how can you tell quickly if your library has these sources? Usually libraries color-code these cards.

▶ **Look at the key below. It shows the color labels placed on cards in a library to indicate media sources. Use it to answer the questions.**

1. You need to make a speech about a famous artist. In your search for the topic "Van Gogh," you find a card with an orange label on it. Will this be useful for your speech? Why?_____

cassette tapes	yellow
CDs	green
videos/DVDs	blue
posters/prints	orange

_____

_____

2. The school poster contest theme is "Sport Safety." Is there a video your teacher can show about the subject? Where would you search in the card catalog? What color label do you need to find? _____

_____

3. Does your library have a video of *Peter Rabbit*? Where would you search in the card catalog? What color label do you need to find? _____

_____

4. Your class plans a story hour for the younger grades. You plan to tell the story of *Little Red Riding Hood,* but you need music with your story. Where would you search in the card catalog? What color label do you need to find? _____

_____

Name That Catalog Card

▶ **Read each sentence below. Decide what type of catalog card will help you find the information quickest. Remember, you may choose a *subject* card, *author* card, or *title* card.**

1. _____ Can you find seven mystery books in your library?

2. _____ Does the library have all the books by Jay T. Book?

3. _____ Can you find the illustrator who drew the pictures for *The Green Caterpillar*?

4. _____ Does the library have 24 books on craft projects, one for each student in your class?

5. _____ Does the library have any ghost stories?

6. _____ Was *Happy Moon* written in 2001?

7. _____ Is there only one book about spiders in the library?

8. _____ Did Greenpond Press publish the book *Green Frogs*?

9. _____ Does your library have more than one book by Sally Q. Bookmark?

10. _____ What is the name of the book about best friends by Juan Rodriguez?

Name That Catalog Card

Read each sentence below. Decide what type of catalog card will help you find the information quickest. Remember, you may choose a *subject* card, *author* card, or *title* card.

1. _____ You need a book about insects for your report. Does the library have any books about insects?

2. _____ Did Henry Buggins write a book about dinosaurs?

3. _____ What books about famous people can you find in the biography section of your library?

4. _____ You heard that *The Day the Plants Talked* is a funny book. Who is the author?

5. _____ Is coral really a sea animal or a plant?

6. _____ Does the library have a book about the solar system by Susan Starlight?

7. _____ Are there any books about Samuel Clemens in your library?

8. _____ Where can you find a book about learning French in your library?

9. _____ Who wrote *The Purple Grasshopper*?

10. _____ Is *The Case of the Yellow Banana* one of several books written by Arthur Spyglass?

Name _____ Date _____

The Electronic Catalog

Libraries use a special organizing system to keep records for all of their books. There is a card for each item in a library. While these can be actual cards about the size of an index card, more often the library catalog is on a computer. You use the **browser station** at your library to search the catalog for a particular item. There are several ways to find a book from the browser station. You can search by:

- **author**   - **title**
- **subject**   - **keyword**

Search Tips

- Remember when you search that you should not count the words *a, an,* or *the.*

- Pay special attention to how your browser asks for information. For example, it may want the *last name* of an author first, then the *first name.*

- Be as specific as you can to narrow your search.

▶ **Use the browser station to search for the following in your school library catalog. Then answer the questions.**

1. Do an author search for E. B. White. How many titles come up?

   List a few titles here. _____

   _____

2. Do a keyword or subject search for "web." How many titles come up?

   List a few titles here. _____

   _____

3. Do a title search for *Charlotte's Web.* How many titles come up? _____

   _____

4. What have you learned about using technology to search based on the

   questions above? _____

   _____

Name _____   Date _____

Title Search

A title search is the most specific of all the searches. There are a few tricks, however, as Talia and Bethany discovered. Talia read a book last summer that she knows Bethany would love. She can't remember the exact title, but knows it has the word "ballet" in it. She thinks the title might be *The Ballet Shoes*, so she types in the following in the title search.

Title Search	the Ballet Shoes

1. What did Talia do that was unnecessary? Explain. _____

_____

2. Does it matter whether you use capital letters when searching? Try it!

_____

▶ **Here are the results of Talia's search. Use it to answer the questions that follow.**

Number	Title	Year
1	Ballet Shoes (videorecording) BBC Enterprises, Ltd.	1990
2	Ballet Shoes / Noel Streatfield Illustrated by Diane Goode	1991
3	Ballet Shoes / Noel Streatfield	1979

3. Talia is sure that the book she read did not have illustrations. Which record should she choose? _____

4. What should Talia and Bethany expect to find if they searched for record 1 on the library shelves? _____

Author Search

You go to your library's browser station and search for the author Jeremy Nutt. Oops! You typed in Jeremy Nutt and didn't get any records. The browser asks for **last name first**, so you retype Nutt, Jeremy. Several books come up, but you select the one you are most interested in—*The Truth About Squirrels.*

► **Here is the record that comes up on your computer screen. Use it to answer the questions that follow.**

Author	Nutt, Jeremy
Title	The truth about squirrels.
Pub Info	New Jersey : Tree Press, c2004.
Description	111 p. illus.
Location (Call #)	599 Nu
Summary	This book tells the facts and fiction about squirrels. Illustrations are large and describe their homes.
Subject	Squirrels—Juvenile literature.

1. What year was the book published? _____

2. What is the call number? _____

3. How many pages are in the book? _____

4. Who is the publisher of the book? Where is that publisher located? _____

_____

5. If you were doing a report about squirrel habitats, would this book be useful?

Explain. _____

_____

Name _____ Date _____

Subject Search

Even though you think squirrels are fun to watch, your dad is going nuts trying to keep them away from the bird feeder. During your library time, you decide to find a book to help him. You aren't sure where to start, so you do a subject search for "squirrels."

Here is what comes up on your computer screen. Use it to answer the questions.

Number	Subjects (1–5 of 5)	Entries Found
1	Squirrels	11
2	Squirrel Control	4
3	Squirrel Humor	3
4	Squirrel Fiction Literature	8
5	Squirrel Sound Recordings	1

1. Which of the subjects above best narrows your search?

_____

2. Which other subject might have helpful information?

_____

After making your selection, another screen comes up. Use it to answer the question that follows.

Subject	**Squirrel Control**	
Number	Title (1–2 of 2)	Year
1	Outwitting Squirrels	2001
2	Techniques for Trapping Squirrels	1987

3. Which of the above titles would you choose to help your dad? Explain.

_____

_____

General and Specific Subjects

▶ **Read the research questions below. Determine if the subjects are *general* or *specific*. Circle the answer. Then tell why you think the question is general or specific.**

environment
endangered
wildlife
extinct

1. What causes wildlife to be endangered or extinct?

general   **specific**

_____

_____

2. Is endangered wildlife found all over the world?

general   **specific**

_____

_____

3. Is the redheaded woodpecker an endangered species?

general   **specific**

_____

_____

4. How do the rain forests affect our environment?

general   **specific**

_____

_____

5. What is a rain forest?

general   **specific**

_____

_____

0-7424-1955-X *Complete Library Skills*

Name _____ Date _____

Use the Funnel

To get the best results when searching, you need to know how wide to make your funnel. What funnel? Look at the example below. Meredith is writing a report on dolphins. So first she types in "dolphins" (a **narrow**, or specific search). She finds a few books but wants to look for more. So she types in "marine animals" (a **broad**, or general search). This results in many more books she might be able to use for her report.

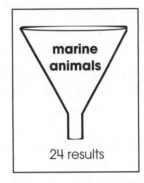
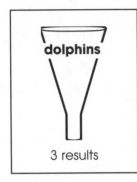

3 results   24 results

▶ **Read the situations below. Write the name of a narrow search in the first funnel. Then write the name of a broad search in the second funnel.**

1. You need a picture of where the planets are in the solar system.

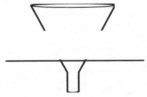

2. Is the ladybug a harmful insect?

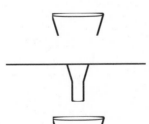
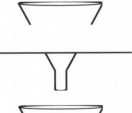

3. Where could you search to find information about baseball?

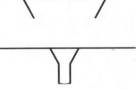

4. You need to find out what to feed your pet guinea pig.

Name _____   Date _____

Keyword Search

Carlos loves to play soccer. He wants to find some soccer books to bring home from his school library. He knows that he should type in the word "soccer," but doesn't know which would be better—a keyword search or a subject search. He decides to try both.

A keyword search returns over 200 records—too many! A subject search returns 75 records—still too many. Since he's not sure of the exact subject he's interested in, he goes back to the keyword search. This time he uses a suggestion on the screen and types "soccer AND training." Aha! This time a list of 8 titles comes up and they are just what he's looking for!

▶ **Answer the questions based on Carlos's experience with searches.**

1. Which appears to be more accurate, a subject search or a keyword search?

_____

2. Why did adding the word "AND" help Carlos's search?

_____

3. What do you think would have happened if Carlos had typed in

"soccer NOT training"? _____

_____

4. A keyword search looks over the entire record for a word, but a subject search only looks in the subject headings for the word. When might a keyword search be more helpful? When might a subject search be more helpful? Explain.

_____

_____

_____

0-7424-1955-X *Complete Library Skills*

Boolean Searches

A Boolean search involves the use of three main terms: **and**, **or**, and **and not**. It is a way to narrow down a keyword search by limiting the results. An example of how a Boolean search works is shown below.

> You need to find information about ecology—specifically about the effects of water pollution on ecology outside the United States. Typing the following keywords into the library's computer, using the Boolean terms **and** and **and not** would get the information needed.

ecology **and** water pollution **and not** United States

Create Boolean searches for the following research questions, using the Boolean terms shown in boldface below. Write your answers on the lines provided.

1. What are the problems of acid rain and the rain forest?

   _____ **or** _____ **and** _____

2. How can you make pizza at home?

   _____ **and** _____ **and not** _____

3. How do you groom a long-haired dog?

   _____ **and** _____ **and not** _____

4. Where can you find information on battery-operated portable CD players?

   _____ **and** _____ **or** _____

Finding Keywords and Search Terms

➡ **Find the keywords to begin computer searches for the research questions below. Then combine keywords to create narrow search terms. Write your answers on the lines provided.**

1. What is the major problem of famous sports stars today?

   keywords: _____

   search terms: _____

2. What do you need to know about packing for a vacation trip?

   keywords: _____

   search terms: _____

3. What do vitamins have to do with nutrition?

   keywords: _____

   search terms: _____

4. How do newspapers explain the events of history?

   keywords: _____

   search terms: _____

5. What do you need to know about caring for a pet?

   keywords: _____

   search terms: _____

6. How do weather patterns in other parts of the world affect the weather in your area?

   keywords: _____

   search terms: _____

Orange You Ready to Search?

➡ **Read each situation below. Decide what type of search will help you. Match each situation to the search that will give the best results. Write the letter on the line.**

1. _____ You heard that *The Orange Who Wore Tennis Shoes* is a funny book. Who is the author?

          a. keyword search "oranges AND cooking"

2. _____ You need to gather a lot of information about oranges for a report. You want to know every book your library has that mentions oranges.

          b. author search "orange"

3. _____ Oranges are on sale at the grocery store. You need some creative recipes using oranges.

          c. subject search "tennis"

4. _____ Your kid brother loves a series of books by somebody named Orange. You want to check one out for him, but don't know the author's first name.

          d. title search *Orange Who Wore Tennis Shoes*

5. _____ The gym teacher is offering free tennis lessons after school. You want to know more about the game of tennis.

          e. keyword search "oranges"

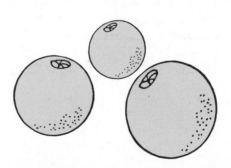

Name _____ Date _____

Extended Searches

Sometimes you have to search further for the information that you need. Each time a new screen appears on the computer monitor, additional "see also" references may be given. By selecting these extended references, you can view additional topics related to your query.

For example, if you are looking for information on how to buy a good set of headphones for your CD player, you might type in "headphones." The screen on the left displays the extended references that are given. You select "portable stereos" and get the screen on the right.

▶ **Use this information to answer the questions on page 25.**

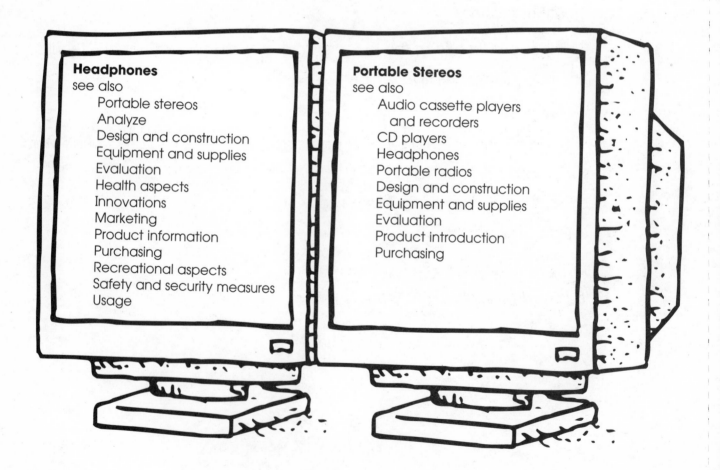

Headphones
see also
　　Portable stereos
　　Analyze
　　Design and construction
　　Equipment and supplies
　　Evaluation
　　Health aspects
　　Innovations
　　Marketing
　　Product information
　　Purchasing
　　Recreational aspects
　　Safety and security measures
　　Usage

Portable Stereos
see also
　　Audio cassette players
　　　and recorders
　　CD players
　　Headphones
　　Portable radios
　　Design and construction
　　Equipment and supplies
　　Evaluation
　　Product introduction
　　Purchasing

Extended Searches (cont.)

Read the research questions on stereo systems listed below. Then review the sample search information on page 24. For each question, find as many categories as you can that could be searched to obtain the needed information. Write your answers on the line.

tape players
stereo headphones
CD players
extended searches

1. Where can you find information on the newest stereo headphones available?

_____

_____

_____

2. Where would you search to find information on how to do simple repairs to a CD player? _____

_____

3. The headphones to your portable CD player are missing one of the padded ear parts. How do you find a replacement? _____

_____

_____

4. You've heard that excessive use of stereo headphones can cause hearing damage. Where can you find the latest information on this? _____

_____

5. Your portable CD player needs new dry-cell batteries. Where can they be bought? _____

_____

Internet Searches

A wealth of information is just a click away. You already know this if you've used the Internet. Searching on the Internet is similar to searching your library's catalog, but the results can include most anything that is out there on the Web. Internet searches use a **search engine** to look for sites that match your words. Your school librarian can help you find the best search engine to use.

See if you can find a web site to answer each of the questions below. First write the words you would use to search. When you find a good site to answer the question, write the name of the site on the line. If you have access to a printer, print each page as you find it.

1. You are doing a project on Spain. You need facts on its capital city, its economy, its flag, and its climate. Where can you find this information? _____

_____

_____

2. Where can you learn what time it is in Greenwich, England?

_____

_____

3. Where can you gather information on the ocelot's diet?

_____

_____

4. Where can you find the rules for the game of chess?

_____

_____

Name _____ Date _____

Internet Searches

➤ **Ask your librarian to help you find the best search engine to use. Then see if you can find a web site to answer each of the questions below. Write the name of the site on the line. If you have access to a printer, print each page as you find it.**

1. Where can you find information on the culture of Native American peoples?

   _____

   _____

   _____

2. What sites will tell you more about the tyrannosaur and its habitat?

   _____

   _____

3. Where can you get information on the ancient Romans and the places they traveled? _____

   _____

4. Where can you find a synonym for the word **difficult**? _____

   _____

   _____

5. How many people live in India and China? _____

   _____

Name _____ Date _____

Evaluating Web Sites as Sources

Not all web sites are created equal. How do you know whether the site you are using is a good source to use for information? First you should think about your **purpose** for searching the web. Are you looking for something fun to do? Are you writing a report for class? It's much more important to use quality sources for a report than it is for something you're doing for fun.

▶ **Study the chart below. It will give you some ideas about what to look for when evaluating web sites. Use it to answer the questions on page 29.**

Good Sources 	Questionable Sources
• accurate; no typing or factual errors • easy to read and understand; graphics are clear and add to the content being discussed • include in-depth information • not biased; contain objective facts • revised frequently; up-to-date • from a reliable source; you've heard of the organization sponsoring the page (a URL ending with **.gov**, **.edu**, or **.org** is also a good sign) • stable; the pages stick around for a long time and are always there when you go back to them	• contain typing errors and errors in fact • difficult to read; graphics are distracting • information is not detailed or in-depth • lots of one person's opinions (very subjective) • page hasn't been revised in a long time • you've never heard of the person or source sponsoring page • here today, gone tomorrow; page is not there when you look for it a few months later

Name _____ Date _____

Evaluating Web Sites as Sources (cont.)

➤ **Use the chart on page 28 to help you answer the questions.**

I. You are trying to find help with converting metric units to customary units. Which of the following web sites would be the best source? Circle your choice. Explain why you picked it on the line below.

a. http://www.joesmathpage.com

b. http://www.library.org/math

c. http://www.icanduemath.com

_____

2. Look at the two screens below. Based on what you see, which is the more reliable source? Circle the source you would use.

a.

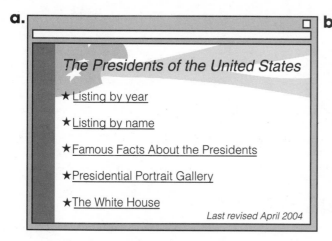

The Presidents of the United States

★ Listing by year

★ Listing by name

★ Famous Facts About the Presidents

★ Presidential Portrait Gallery

★ The White House

Last revised April 2004

b.

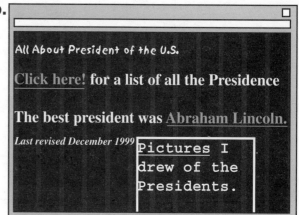

All About President of the U.S.

Click here! for a list of all the Presidence

The best president was Abraham Lincoln.

Last revised December 1999

Pictures I drew of the Presidents.

3. Your friend Anthony needs help finding information for a report. He wants to use the Internet, but doesn't even know where to begin. Make a "Best of the Web" list for Anthony of the four most reputable sources you know to find information. You may ask your teacher or school librarian to help get you started.
Write the URLs on the lines below.

_____   _____

_____   _____

Can You Spy the Best Site?

▶ **Read each of the research situations presented here and on page 31. Determine which of the web sites listed would be the best source of information. More than one site may sound appealing, but you are to choose the best and most reliable source. (Look back at the chart on page 28 for help on evaluating sources.) Circle the letter of your choice. Then write why you chose that site on the lines below.**

1. You are writing a report about lions and are looking for

   some facts about lions kept in zoos.

   a. The National Zoo

   http://natzoo.si.edu

   b. Lucy's Lion Lovers Page

   http://www.lucyluvslions.com

   c. National Aquarium

   http://www.aqua.org

   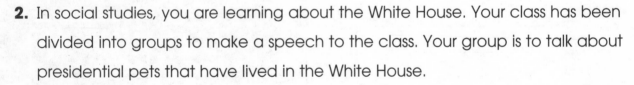

   _____

   _____

2. In social studies, you are learning about the White House. Your class has been

   divided into groups to make a speech to the class. Your group is to talk about

   presidential pets that have lived in the White House.

   a. White House Pets

   http://www.homepage.com/jrolfe/pets

   b. Dogs in the White House

   http://mysite.presidentdogs.com

   c. The White House

   http://www.whitehouse.gov/kids/

   _____

   _____

Name _____ Date _____

Using an Almanac

▶ **Do this math problem to come up with your "Year to Remember." Next, find the almanac for that year and fill in the information below.**

Math Problem

_ _ _ _ Take the year you were born and

+10 _ _ _ _ add ten years.

- 3 _ _ _ _ Subtract three years.

Write the result on the line below.

= _ _ _ _ **A Year to Remember**

Sports

Who won the World Series? _____

Who won the Super Bowl? _____

Government

Who was the President? _____

Who was governor of your state? _____

Entertainment

What was voted best movie? _____

Name the top TV show. _____

News

What were the top two news stories? _____

Vital Statistics

How many births in the U.S. that year? _____

How many deaths? _____

Going to Extremes

► **Where can you find answers to the following extreme questions? Use your reference section to fill in the answers. Then write the letters in order in the circles across the bottom to find the answer.**

1. What is the world's largest animal?

   — — — —   — — ◯ — —

2. What city is home to the world's tallest building?

   — — — ◯ — — — — — — —

3. What is the fastest planet in our solar system?

   ◯ — — — — — —

4. Which country in the world has the most people?

   — — — — ◯

5. What country is home to the world's longest bridge?

   — — — ◯

6. Where would you find the smallest bone in your body?

   — ◯ —

7. What is the most populous state in the United States?

   ◯ — — — — — — — — — —

8. Where could you find the answers to these extreme questions?

   ◯ ◯ ◯ ◯ ◯ ◯ ◯

Name _____   Date _____

Know-It-All-Manac

➡ **Use an almanac to help you answer the questions below.**

1. What is the current population of your state?

_____

2. Who are two people in the Baseball Hall of Fame?

_____

3. Name three instruments in the woodwind family.

_____

4. What author won the Newbery Medal this year?

_____

5. Which planet has the most moons?

_____

6. Which President had the shortest presidency?

_____

7. Who won the Super Bowl this year?

_____

8. What is the world's largest continent?

_____

Using an Atlas

An **atlas** is a book of maps. Sometimes it contains maps of an entire country, sometimes the whole world, sometimes just maps for a particular state.

Tabitha's family is going to Springfield, Illinois. On the map next to the name of the city, she found the code **H-5.** The **H** represents the letters along the side of the map. The **5** represents the numbers along the bottom of the map.

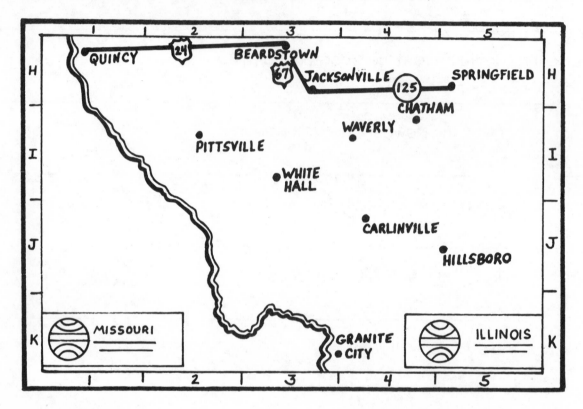

▶ **Write the correct code next to each city listed below.**

1. Jacksonville _____   **2.** Carlinville _____

3. Pittsville _____   **4.** Beardstown _____

5. Quincy _____   **6.** Chatham _____

7. White Hall _____   **8.** Granite City _____

Name _____ Date _____

That's Just Capital

➤ **Use an atlas to help you match each capital city to the correct country. Write the letter on the line.**

1. _____ Canberra
2. _____ Brussels
3. _____ Accra
4. _____ Bucharest
5. _____ Seoul
6. _____ Oslo
7. _____ Ottawa
8. _____ Buenos Aires
9. _____ Hanoi
10. _____ Madrid

a. Norway
b. South Korea
c. Canada
d. Vietnam
e. Belgium
f. Spain
g. Australia
h. Ghana
i. Romania
j. Argentina

Answers Down Under

Turn to the index in an **atlas** and find
the pages listed under "Australia."
You will need to find the **legend** (or **key**)
for the different maps of Australia.
The legend will help you read each map.

▶ **Use maps of Australia to answer the following questions.**

1. Name the provinces and territories in Australia. _____

_____

2. What do you notice about where the major cities in Australia are located?

_____

3. The largest area of Australia is used for what? (Hint: Use the economic/

mineral map.) _____

4. How many time zones does Australia have? _____

5. Using the climate (environment) map, describe the large center area of

Australia. _____

_____

6. Name two oceans that surround Australia. _____

_____

7. On which side of Australia is the Great Barrier Reef located

(north, south, east, or west)? _____

8. What is the name of the island state off the southern coast of Australia?

_____

Reference Guide Words

Reference books have **guide words** at the top of each page. The two words give you a clue about what other words or topics you will find on the page. The word on the left-hand side is always the first word on the page. The word on the right-hand side is the last word on the page.

▶ **Use the Word Box to write each word on the correct page in alphabetical order.**

Word Box			
arch	anteater	always	apple
action	after	animal	attention

Encyclopedias

Encyclopedias can either be **electronic** (on the computer) or **bound** (books on the shelf). Bound encyclopedias are arranged in alphabetical order and come in many volumes. Encyclopedias contain facts on people, places, things, events, and other topics. When you first begin looking up information on a subject, the encyclopedia is a good place to start because it gives you a broad **overview** of the subject. If you want to find out more than just general information about something, you should also check books, magazines, newspapers, and other sources in addition to the encyclopedia.

There are some important rules to remember when looking up a topic in the encyclopedia.

- Look for the last name of a person.

- For a titled person, look under the name, not the title.

- In words of two or more parts that are not the names of people, look for the first part.

- For an abbreviation, look for the word as though it were spelled in full.

▶ **Imagine that you are getting ready to do some research in the library. Look at each topic below. Underline the word for which you would look in an encyclopedia. Then, using the encyclopedias below, write the volume number where you would find that topic on the line.**

_____ **1.** Ms. Molly Pitcher

_____ **2.** New York

_____ **3.** Mt. Rushmore

_____ **4.** Native Americans

_____ **5.** Marco Polo

_____ **6.** Monroe Doctrine

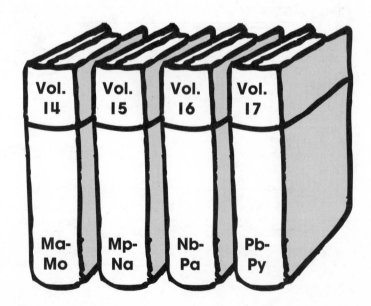

Vol. 14 — Ma-Mo Vol. 15 — Mp-Na Vol. 16 — Nb-Pa Vol. 17 — Pb-Py

The Encyclopedia Index

The **index** is usually the last book or volume in an encyclopedia set and it lists all of the subjects that are covered in the entire set. Indexes will give the **volume** and **page number** for each topic.

▶ **Study the entry for *Leaf* in the sample entry below from an encyclopedia index. Then answer the questions.**

Leaf (botany)	L:151 *with pictures*
Bud	B:675 *with pictures*
Deciduous tree	D:70
Fern (parts of a fern)	F:74 *with pictures*
Grass (the grass plant)	G:434
Photosynthesis	P:434
Plant (leaves)	P:536 *with pictures*
Transpiration	T:379
Tree	T:410 (leaves)
Vegetable (leaves)	V:310 *with pictures*

1. Can you find a picture of the grass plant? If so, name the page number. _____

2. Where might you find information about the leaves of trees? Name the volume and page numbers. _____

3. Where might you find information about the leaf bud and leaf fern? Name the volume and page numbers. _____

4. You need to know about plant leaves. Can this encyclopedia help you? How do you know? _____

   _____

5. You need information about plants you can eat. Will this encyclopedia help you? What volume and page number? _____

   _____

Comparing Encyclopedia Indexes

▶ The following entries for *Dinosaurs* come from two different encyclopedias.
Use them to answer the questions on page 51.

Science Times Encyclopedia

Dinosaurs

fossils	F 123–131
how dinosaurs found food	D 117–120
how dinosaurs lived	D 121–123
how and why dinosaurs disappeared	D 125–126
poems about dinosaurs	P 107

World of Science Encyclopedia

Dinosaurs

bones	B:124–129
flying ancient animals (pictures)	F:138
fossils (pictures)	F:37
glaciers and dinosaurs	G:334–339
prehistoric animals	P:111

Comparing Encyclopedia Indexes (cont.)

▶ **Study the entry for *Dinosaurs* in each of the encyclopedia indexes listed on page 50. Use them to answer the questions. Write the name of the encyclopedia, volume, and page number that you would go to for information.**

1. Did glaciers have anything to do with the disappearance of the dinosaur?

_____

2. How did the dinosaurs disappear? _____

_____

3. Can you find a picture of dinosaur fossils? _____

_____

4. Are there any poems about dinosaurs? _____

_____

5. What did dinosaurs eat? _____

_____

6. Is the dinosaur the largest prehistoric animal that ever lived? _____

_____

7. What was the dinosaur's daily life like? _____

_____

8. Did dinosaurs ever fly? _____

_____

Name _____ Date _____

Using Headings

When you read an encyclopedia article, you may find that there is a great deal of information for you to read. If you are writing a report, it may take you a long time to sort through it all. Encyclopedia **headings** can help you. They divide the article into parts. They work as book chapters do. You need not read an entire encyclopedia article to find information. Skim or read the headings. They will tell you what is in that part of the article.

Study the headings and subheadings in the sample entry below. Use them to answer the questions on page 53.

Dinosaurs (a)

Time of the Dinosaurs (b)
The Dinosaur and Where It Lived
Plant Life During Time of the Dinosaur
Animal Life During Time of the Dinosaur
Land and Climate During the Time of the Dinosaur

Kinds of Dinosaurs (c)
Large
Small
Flying

How Dinosaurs Lived (d)
Getting Food
Protection Against Enemies

Working with Dinosaur Fossils (e)
Finding Fossils
Digging Fossils
Fossils and Museums

Name _____ Date _____

Using Headings (cont.)

➤ **Refer to the sample entry on *Dinosaurs* on page 52. Write the letter of the heading that will help you answer the questions. You may need to use more than one letter for each question.**

1. _____ You need information for your report about how fossils are displayed in museums.

2. _____ Each member of your group will write a chapter about dinosaurs. Your topic is dinosaur bones and fossils.

3. _____ Did dinosaurs disappear because of their enemies?

4. _____ Did dinosaurs ever eat tree leaves?

5. _____ What were weather conditions like during the time of the dinosaur?

6. _____ Did dinosaurs like any special type of area for their homes?

7. _____ Did dinosaurs ever eat other animals?

8. _____ How did scientists remove fossils from the earth?

9. _____ Did dinosaurs ever fly?

10. _____ What can you find out about dinosaurs and museums?

Name _____ Date _____

Using Subheadings

Often an encyclopedia article has many pages on a single topic. Encyclopedia **headings** and **subheadings** can help you locate information quickly. They can also let you know if the information you need will be covered by a particular section in the article.

► **Use the sample headings and subheadings below to answer the questions on page 55.**

Kites (a)

How Kites Fly (b)

Types of Kites (c)
    Flat Kite **(d)**
    Bowed Kite **(e)**
    Box Kite **(f)**
    Flying Kite **(g)**
    Triangular Kite **(h)**

History of the Kite (i)
    Early Kites **(j)**
    In China **(k)**
    In Europe **(l)**
    In America **(m)**

Uses of Kites (n)
    In Government **(o)**
    In Weather Forecasting **(p)**
    In Science Experiments **(q)**

Using Subheadings (cont.)

Refer to the sample entry on *Kites* on page 54. Write the letter of the heading or subheading that will help you answer the questions. You may need to use more than one letter for each question.

1. _____ Did the first kite to fly have a triangular shape?

2. _____ Did the Chinese invent the kite?

3. _____ You need to know how to build a kite so that it will fly.

4. _____ Were kites ever used by governments?

5. _____ You plan to write a report about the kite in other countries.

6. _____ How are kites used in America?

7. _____ Are kites ever used to predict what the weather will be like?

8. _____ You plan to give a talk about the different kinds of kites.

9. _____ Are kites ever used in Europe?

10. _____ You plan a report about the types of kites and how to build them.

"See Also" References

Let's say that you find the encyclopedia you need. You find the page of the article you need. You read the article, but you could use more information. Where do you go? At the end of the encyclopedia article is a list of subjects. Not every article will have them, but if it does, you will see the words **see also**. "See also" references tell you where you can find other encyclopedia articles. These articles are related to the subject of the article. If you know how to use "see also" references, you can save time searching for information.

▶ **Study the sample entries below. Use them to answer the questions on page 57.**

Airplane. *See also* airplane (models); helicopter; Wright Brothers; test pilots.

Amphibian. *See also* frog; toad; salamander.

Animals. *See also* nature study; pets; wildlife; zoos; protective coloring.

Ant. *See also* anteater; insect; termite.

Antennae. *See also* ant (sense); bee (body of the honey bee);
    insect (senses of insects); beetle (bodies of beetles); butterfly (the head).

Apple. *See also* cider; fruit (chart of leading fruits); tree (picture).

Astronaut. *See also* space travel; Cape Canaveral; Armstrong, Neal; Glenn, John.

Astronomy. *See also* stars; constellation; galaxy; Halley's Comet; space travel.

Atlas. *See also* maps (how they are made).

Automobile. *See also* automobile industry (pictures); automobile
    models (hobby).

"See Also" References (cont.)

➤ **Use the sample entries on page 56 to fill in the blanks.**

1. You plan a report about space travel.

   Most of your report will be about the astronauts.

   See **astronaut** and see also _____ ,

   _____ , and _____ .

2. Your teacher started a unit on objects in space. Where can you find more information about Halley's Comet? See **astronomy** and see also

   _____ .

3. Your report about animals needs more information. You plan to write about animals in zoos. See **animals** and see also _____ and

   _____ .

4. You volunteered to make cider for the class project. You know that you begin with apples. See **apples** and see also _____ .

5. You plan to get your cousin a model kit for his birthday, but you need an idea of the different kinds of cars. See **automobiles** and see also _____ .

6. One of your grandfather's hobbies is airplanes. You want to find out more about the first people connected with airplanes. See **airplanes** and see also

   _____ and _____ .

7. Your class is studying insects. The last chapter discussed how an antenna works. What information can you find about **antennae**? See _____

   and see also _____ , _____ ,

   and _____ .

Name _____ Date _____

Using Specialized Encyclopedias

Encyclopedias cover a wide range of topics, but **specialized encyclopedias** cover a wide range of information about one large topic. Often they can shorten your research time by giving you more detailed information than a general encyclopedia.

> *The Encyclopedia of Inventions*
>
> *The Encyclopedia of Hobbies*
>
> *The Collectibles Encyclopedia*
>
> *American Encyclopedia of History*
>
> *Science Encyclopedia of Today*
>
> *Art Today Encyclopedia*

▶ **Read the report topics. Which specialized encyclopedia in the list above might give you useful information?**

1. black holes _____

2. Civil War _____

3. how the cotton gin works _____

4. Van Gogh and impressionism _____

5. stamp collections _____

6. quasars _____

7. abstract art _____

8. whaling industry in early America _____

Using Specialized Encyclopedias

➤ **Read the report topics. Which specialized encyclopedia from the list below might give you useful information?**

Encyclopedia of Sports	*Encyclopedia of Inventions*
Art in America	*Encyclopedia of Science*
Encyclopedia of World History	*Space and Star Encyclopedia*
Hobby Master Encyclopedia	*The Collectibles Encyclopedia*

1. early explorers _____

2. landscape painters _____

3. latest discoveries _____

4. African history _____

5. history of soccer _____

6. movie pictures _____

7. satellites _____

8. Australian colonization _____

9. postcards _____

10. model airplanes _____

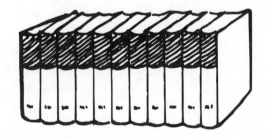

Dictionary Skills

The **dictionary** is a book that contains a list of words in alphabetical order. You can use the dictionary for many things.

- spelling of a word
- meaning of a word
- pronunciation of a word
- syllables in a word
- part(s) of speech

dic·tion·ar·y \ ˈdik-sh(ə)-ner-ē \ *noun*

a book that lists the words of a language in alphabetical order, along with information about their meaning, spelling, and pronunciation

To find your way around in a dictionary, you need to be able to use the **guide words** on the upper corner of each page. Only words that come between them in alphabetical order are on that page. The first guide word will be the first entry on the page. The second guide word will be the last entry on the page.

 Draw a line to match each entry word to the correct guide words.

Entry Word	Guide Words
1. blackberry	baffle–barge
2. coconut	canopy–chirp
3. cherry	chisel–choir
4. chocolate	bison–blackbird
5. banana	city–crash

Parts of Speech

▶ **Use the sample dictionary entries below to identify the correct part of speech for each underlined word. Write the answer on the line.**

---

chime \'chīm\ *noun* 1. a set of bells 2. the sound of bells

verb 1. to make a musical sound

slick \'slik\ *noun* 1. something that is slippery 2. a film of oil

verb 1. to make smooth or slippery *adjective* 1. slippery 2. clever

yellow \'yel ō\ *noun* 1. a color like a lemon *verb* 1. to become
yellow *adjective* 1. of the color yellow 2. cowardly

---

1. _____ Pearl heard the clock <u>chime</u> six o'clock.

2. _____ I sat in a <u>yellow</u> chair in the doctor's office.

3. _____ We walked carefully because the sidewalk was <u>slick</u> after the rain.

4. _____ Angelica <u>slicked</u> back her hair for the play.

5. _____ A green banana will <u>yellow</u> in a few days.

6. _____ Mr. Tamara heard the <u>chime</u> sounding in the wind.

7. _____ That new detective is one <u>slick</u> fellow.

8. _____ My <u>yellow</u> dog was afraid to jump in the water.

Name _____ Date _____

Syllagraph

► **Shade in the graph to show the number of syllables in each word. Use your dictionary to help you.**

	1	2	3	4
watermelon				
breakfast				
servant				
buffalo				
arch				
aggressive				
victim				
column				
history				
significant				
margin				
debilitate				
pilot				
compulsory				
cucumber				
leisure				
sketch				
traditional				
conventional				

Number of Syllables

► **Choose two 3-syllable words from the list above. Write the words on the blanks. Show each syllable separated by a dash. Check your answers in the dictionary and write the page number of the entry on the blank.**

Word	Syllables	Page
_____	_____	_____
_____	_____	_____

Multiple Madness

▶ **Use the sample entry to answer the questions.**

> **block** \blok\ *noun* 1. a piece of wood 2. a platform from which property is sold at auction 3. a football play 4. a mold on which items are shaped 5. a line of houses enclosed by streets *verb* 1. to keep from passing 2. to shut off from view

1. How many noun definitions are given for *block*? _____

2. How may verb definitions are given for *block*? _____

3. How many definitions all together in this entry for *block*? _____

▶ **Write the part of speech and correct definition for *block* on the lines.**

4. Thick trees <u>block</u> the sun from the forest floor. _____

_____

5. Seth lives on the same <u>block</u> as I do. _____

_____

▶ **Write a sentence using the following definitions of *block*.**

6. the second noun definition _____

_____

7. the first verb definition _____

_____

Phonetic Spelling

A dictionary not only tells you the meaning of a word, but also how to pronounce it. Dictionaries use the **phonetic spelling** to show how a word is said. You can look in the front of your dictionary for an explanation of phonetic symbols and how to pronounce them.

▶ **Decode the passage. Write the correct spelling of each word in the blank. Do you know the answer?**

Frum insīde cāvz and binēth _____

brijez, thēz flīing krēcherz _____

kum out. Apēring at nĭt, _____

thā lŏŏk fawr fōŏd, diping _____

and dīving ebout. Thā _____

sē with ther ērz and _____

nät ther īz. Dŏŏ yŏŏ nō _____

the mamel in this disgīz? _____

What is this animal? _____

The Biographical Dictionary

A **biographical dictionary** is a special kind of dictionary. It is a dictionary of people. When you have no information on a person, the biographical dictionary will give you a starting place to find out when a person lived and what they did. The names in a biographical dictionary are arranged alphabetically by **last name**.

▶ **Below is a sample entry from a biographical dictionary. Use it to answer the following questions.**

> **Buchanan, Sir George.** 1831–1895. English physician and exponent of sanitary science. Chief agent in eradicating typhus fever, reducing mortality from tuberculosis, and controlling cholera. His eldest son, Sir George Seaton (1869–1936), hygienist, was senior medical officer, Ministry of Health (1919–1934).
>
> **Buchanan, Sir George Cunningham.** 1865–1940. British civil engineer, specialist in harbor, dock, and river works.
>
> **Buchanan, Sir George William.** 1854–1924. British diplomatist of Scottish family; ambassador at St. Petersburg (1910–1918).

1. From what country is Sir George William Buchanan? _____

2. When did George Cunningham Buchanan die? _____

3. What occupation did Sir George Buchanan have? _____

4. Which of the Buchanans listed above was born first? _____

5. You want to find out more about Sir George Buchanan. Where might you look for further information? Under what subjects might you search? _____

_____

_____

Using the Biographical Dictionary

➡ **Use a biographical dictionary to answer the questions.**

1. What is Miguel de Cervantes' most famous work? _____

_____

2. When did Napoleon Bonaparte die? _____

3. What was the occupation of Ida B. Wells? _____

4. What was the occupation of Zheng He? _____

5. When was Martin Luther born? _____

6. What song is Julia Ward Howe famous for writing? _____

7. What were three of George Washington Carver's occupations? _____

_____

8. What nationality was Filippo Brunelleschi? _____

9. What is Jane Addams known for? _____

_____

10. When was Leonardo da Vinci born? _____

11. When did Harriet Tubman die? _____

12. What nationality was Shogun Minamoto Yoritomo? _____

Using a Thesaurus

A **thesaurus** is a book of synonyms (words that have almost the same meaning). A thesaurus can give you new choices for words instead of using the same words over and over again. A thesaurus can help you pick the best word to write.

▶ **Spice up this paragraph! Use a thesaurus to find replacements for the underlined words in the passage below. Write at least two different choices for each word on the lines below.**

My best friend is so <u>nice</u>. I struck out so many times during the softball game I felt <u>bad</u>. The sun was so <u>bright</u> in my eyes I had a hard time keeping my eye on the ball. Even when I got <u>afraid</u> to bat again, my friend cheered me on from the stands. "<u>Good</u> job," she said. "You didn't give up!" Then after the game, we went out for some <u>tasty</u> ice cream. Even though I felt <u>sad</u> about the way the game went, the ice cream made me feel better. Everyone should have a friend who is so <u>great</u>.

Word	Replacement Words	
nice	_____	_____
bad	_____	_____
bright	_____	_____
afraid	_____	_____
good	_____	_____
tasty	_____	_____
sad	_____	_____
great	_____	_____

Parts of a Book

Everything you see is made of parts. A bicycle, a car, a television, and a stereo are all made of smaller units. A book is no exception; each of its parts helps the book work as a whole. Look at the **cover** of a book; what do you see? You see the title, author, and possibly the illustrator's name. Now open the book and turn to the **title and copyright page**. They present the full title of the book, the author, the year of publication, and the publisher. The **table of contents** gives an overview of what you will find in the book with the page numbers for each section. The book might have a preface. Not all books have a **preface**, but if a book does have one, it is usually very short. It explains the important facts or thoughts the author wants you to know.

The main part of the book is called the **body** of the book. This is "the book"; it has all the information you will need. The body is the largest part of the book. At the back of the book there may be an **appendix**. This is information the author would like you to refer to in the book. Rather than include long charts or explanations within the body of a book, the author may collect it in an appendix. A **glossary** may follow these pages. A glossary is like a mini-dictionary that lists in alphabetical order all the important terms presented in the book. The **index** is the last part of a book. It is an alphabetical listing of all key subjects discussed in the book with the page number where each is found.

▶ **Match each part of a book to its correct description. Write the letter on the line before each term.**

1. _____ copyright page   **a.** alphabetical list of terms with definitions

2. _____ table of contents   **b.** alphabetical list of subjects with page numbers

3. _____ glossary   **c.** explains important facts the author wants you to know

4. _____ index   **d.** includes author's name and year of publication

5. _____ preface   **e.** overview of what is in the book (includes page numbers)

Copyright Page

What information does the copyright page include and why is it important? This page tells you when the book was copyrighted. What does this mean? Think of a **copyright date** as the official "birth date" of a book. Why is it so important to know what the copyright date of a book is? Let's say you are writing about computers and have two possible books to use as sources. One book has a copyright date of 1991, and the other has a date of 2001. The 2001 book would have more recent information. Other times you might be more interested in an older book. Say you were writing a report about the history of developments in space travel. A book with an earlier copyright date would tell you how people thought about developments at the time and how they imagined space travel might be in the future. You could compare what their predictions were with what actually happened. Do you see why the copyright page can be helpful to you?

Other important information that is on the copyright page is the **place of publication** and **name of the publisher**. When you are writing information about your sources at the end of your report (the bibliography), you will need to include this information as part of your citation.

▶ **Read the following statements about copyright pages. Write a *T* if the statement is true and an *F* if the statement is false.**

1. _____ You could find the chapter titles on a copyright page.

2. _____ The copyright page could help you find the book with the latest information.

3. _____ The copyright page includes information you need for a bibliography.

4. _____ You would never want to use a book with an older copyright page.

5. _____ The copyright date is like a birth date for a book.

Using the Title and Copyright Pages

▶ **Use the sample title and copyright pages below to answer the questions on page 71.**

The Case of
the Purple Shoes

by Harriet B. Sole
Illustrated by Linda Heel Toe

Mystery Press
Strangetown, New Jersey

Copyright © 1999 by Mystery Press
Strangetown, New Jersey 07778

Today's Trends
in
Footwear

by
Solly N. Sneaker

Infomatic Publications

Copyright © 2003
by Infomatic Publications
Sandals, California

Using the Title and Copyright Pages (cont.)

▶ **Use the sample title and copyright pages on page 70 to answer the questions below.**

1. What year was *The Case of the Purple Shoes* published? _____

2. Where is Infomatic Publications located? _____

3. Which book would you be more likely to use for a report on what today's kids like to wear on their feet? Why? _____

_____

4. Every time you read a book, your little brother likes to peek over your shoulders and look at the pictures. Which book would he rather you chose? _____

_____

5. Harriet B. Sole is one of your favorite authors and you want to send a letter to her publisher. Do you have enough information to do that? Explain.

_____

6. Who is Linda Heel Toe? _____

7. On a scrap of paper you have copied a funny paragraph about shoes. You plan to use it in your report, so you need information for the bibliography. You can't remember which book you used, but you do have these words written on the paper—"Sandals, CA, 2003, Sneaker." Which book was the source for the paragraph? _____

_____

8. Would *Today's Trends in Footwear* be a good book to check if you wanted to know the history of shoes? Why or why not? _____

_____

_____

Table of Contents

The **table of contents** follows the title and copyright pages. It can give you important information quickly and easily. The table of contents gives you a **general idea** of what is in the book by giving you the titles of the chapters or sections.

How can a table of contents help you? Let's say that you are writing a report about ants. You stand before the science shelves in your library and see ten books about ants. How do you find out which books will help you without reading them all? You use the table of contents in each book.

 Compare the table of contents pages from two different books about ants. Use them to answer the questions that follow.

Contents for Book A	Contents for Book B
Chapter 1 What is an ant?	1 The ant's body parts
Chapter 2 Why ants build colonies	2 Types of ants
Chapter 3 How ants build colonies	3 Where ants are found in the world
Chapter 4 What ants eat	4 What ants eat

1. Suppose your report about ants will be about how they build their colonies. Which of the above books will be helpful? How do you know? _____

_____

2. Would you check Book B out of the library? Why or why not? _____

_____

3. Is the title of a book enough to decide whether it will have the information you need? Explain. _____

_____

Name _____ Date _____

Using the Table of Contents

Reading a table of contents will help you find information you need about a particular subject. Look at the following sample table of contents from a book about earthquakes.

Table of Contents

Cracks and Faults	page 4
Continental Drifting	page 22
Earthquakes in the Ocean	page 30
Measuring Earthquakes	page 45
Most Damaging Earthquakes in History	page 61
Earthquake Prediction	page 78
Protection from Earthquakes	page 89
Preventing Earthquakes	page 103

▶ **Write the page number of the chapter that would most likely contain information about the topics listed below.**

1. the earthquake that caused the most damage   _____

2. instruments that signal an earthquake is on the way   _____

3. where the continents have split and moved apart   _____

4. what builders have done to keep buildings safe   _____

5. the scale used to tell how bad an earthquake is   _____

6. the difference between cracks and faults   _____

Name _____ Date _____

Index

An index is a list of topics or subjects in alphabetical order. The index is found at the very back of a book, in the very last volume of an encyclopedia, or the front page of a newspaper. An **index** gives **detailed information**, so it is much longer than a table of contents. A table of contents gives general information.

Imagine that your teacher has assigned each student to research an animal's home. Your report will be about how ants build their colonies. You see ten books about ants on the shelf. Do you read all ten books? You can first read the table of contents in each book. There may be a whole chapter on colony building. Or maybe there is only one small paragraph about colonies in the entire book. How do you find out? Use the index at the back of the book.

 Use the sample index entry to answer the questions below.

> horses
> breeds, 24, 34
> competitions, 51–52
> exercising, 39–42

1. You are writing about horses and are ready to include information about how to exercise a horse. Based on the index entry above, would this book be helpful to you? _____

   How many pages of information would this book have for your report? _____

2. Your friend Joanna enters in many riding shows. Her entire report is going to be about showing horses at competitions. Will this book be useful for her? Why or why not? _____

   _____

3. On how many pages could you find information about horse breeds? _____
   (Hint: What is the difference between a comma between entries and a dash?)

Name _____ Date _____

The Index Page

Afghan hounds	20, 24	breeds of dogs, special	27
American Kennel Club	19	eyesight	22
avalanche rescue dogs	20–21	face language	28
basset hound	27, 31	guide dogs	27
beauty parlors for dogs	31	hearing, sense of	22
breeds of dogs and their		puppies	24–26
ancestors	23	rescue dogs	25
breeds of dogs, illustrated	24–25	tail language	34
breeds of dogs, number of	19	training dogs	58

▶ **You are looking for information about dogs. Check the book index above. Use it to answer the questions.**

1. What pages will give you information about rescue dogs? _____

2. On what page can you find information about the number of dog breeds? _____

3. Can you find information about caring for puppies? If so, on what page? _____

4. Is there any information about a dog's sense of taste? If so, on what page? _____

5. Can you find information about the history of dogs? If so, on what page? _____

6. What three listings give information about how dogs can be useful to help humans? _____

_____

7. What listing will give you pictures of what different dogs look like? _____

8. Where can you find information about what people do to pamper their dogs and make them beautiful? _____

 0-7424-1955-X *Complete Library Skills*

Using a Book Index

Ants	
ants, body parts	p. 3, 37, 40
ants, brown	p. 17, 39
ants, enemies	p. 31, 32, 33
ants, food	p. 5, 6, 7
ants, homes	p. 39–42
ants, places found throughout the world	p. 117–123
ants, red	p. 3
ants, and spiders	p. 67–71
ants, and termites	p. 87
ants, their helpfulness to people	p. 89–94

▶ **Where would you expect to find information to answer the following questions? Give a page number or the name of the listing.**

1. You need information about ants and the desert. Can ants be found in deserts or dry climates? _____

2. You are drawing a cover for your report about ants. You plan to color in at least two types of ants. What two listings will help you? _____

3. Your cousin is studying ant hills. How do ants build ant hills? Where do you look? _____

4. Do ants ever eat green leaves? Where do you look? _____

5. Your little brother is just about to step on an ant hill. "Stop that!" you warn. "Don't you know that ants help people?" What listing will give you more facts? _____

6. How are ants and termites different? _____

Using a Book Index

Ants

ants, the body	p. 5
ants, the colony	p. 7
ants, food	p. 13
ants, location of the colony	p. 15
ants, and people	p. 9
ants, queen	p. 23
ants, their enemies	p. 27
ants, types	p. 17
ants, and the weather	p. 31
ants, worker	p. 19

Read the following questions. You can find where to get the answers by reading the book index. Some questions will have more than one page number for an answer.

1. On what pages can you find information about the places where ants might make their colonies? _____

2. Is a drone a type of ant? _____

3. Are spiders friendly with ants? _____

4. Are green plants a good food source for ants? _____

5. Does an ant have three major body parts or more? _____

6. What is the difference between red and brown ants? _____

7. What is the difference between a worker and a queen ant? _____

8. How do cold temperatures and snow affect ants? _____

Comparing Contents and Index Pages

It is important to understand the difference between the table of contents and the index. You will use the **table of contents** when you are interested in a **general** piece of information. You will use the **index** when you want a **specific** piece of information.

▶ **Use the sample contents and index below to answer the questions on page 79.**

Contents

Chapter 1   What Is a Bee?

Chapter 2   How Bees Live

Chapter 3   Workers

Chapter 4   Queens and Drones

Chapter 5   More Bees

Index

antennae	8
abdomen	8, 25
beeswax	12, 34
body	8
bumblebee	11
colony	10, 38
comb	19
drone	12, 28, 34, 36, 38
eggs	29, 33, 34, 36
feelers	8
glands	8, 34
hive	10, 38
larva	34, 36
nectar	22, 24
pollen	8, 20, 21
pupa	36
queen	12, 30, 33, 35, 37–38
royal jelly	35
scouts	14
sting	8, 25
stomach	23
swarm	14–16

Comparing Contents and Index Pages (cont.)

➤ **Refer to the sample contents and index on page 78. Circle the best place to start looking for the information given—the table of contents or the index. If your answer is "index," write the page number where the information would be found.**

1. How do bees make wax?

      table of contents   **index**   _____

2. You need an overview of how the queen bee and drones work together.

      table of contents   **index**   _____

3. Is there such a thing as scout bees?

      table of contents   **index**   _____

4. You need to know about bees and pollen.

      table of contents   **index**   _____

5. You need a lot of information about how bees live in their hive.

      table of contents   **index**   _____

6. What happens when bees sting?

      table of contents   **index**   _____

7. Why do bees swarm?

      table of contents   **index**   _____

8. How is a bumblebee different from a regular bee?

      table of contents   **index**   _____

Glossary

What is a **glossary**? Where do you find it in a book? A glossary is like a **mini-dictionary** for the new or difficult words in the book. You will find it at the back of the book. It is in alphabetical order. This book contains a glossary on pages 122–123.

When do you use a glossary? You can use it several ways. Let's say that you do not understand a word you wrote in your notes. You are writing about the habits of the brown ant. The book used the word **antennae**. You wrote it down, but forgot to explain what it was. How can you get that information quickly? Check the glossary. It will define the word for you.

➤ **Use the sample glossary entries below from a book about basketball to answer the questions.**

> **tipoff**—when players jump up to tip the ball to their team at the start of a game (or overtime period)
>
> **traveling**—walking more than one step while holding the ball
>
> **turnover**—when a team loses possession of the ball before trying to get a basket

1. If a referee calls a player for "traveling," what was the player doing?

_____

2. Why would it be bad for a team to have lots of turnovers?

_____

3. If you were looking for a definition of "shot clock," would you look before or after these entries? Why? _____

_____

Using the Glossary

➤ **A glossary is a mini-dictionary found at the back of the book. Use the glossary on pages 122–123 to answer the following questions.**

1. What is the difference between a **keyword** and **search terms**?

_____

_____

2. Where in a book would you find a **preface**? Where would you find

an **appendix**? _____

_____

3. How is a **glossary** different from an **index**? _____

_____

_____

4. Which gives more detailed information—an **index** or a **table of contents**?

_____

5. What is the difference between an encyclopedia **see also** reference and

a **heading**? _____

_____

6. What information does a **bibliography** give? _____

_____

7. What is the difference between a **card catalog** and **browser station**?

_____

8. What is the purpose of **guide letters**? _____

_____

Name _____ Date _____

Magazines

There are many children's magazines. Some are specialized to cover topics in science, history, or literature, while others contain more general information. Reading a magazine may be a refreshing change from reading a whole book. With a magazine you can start and finish a story or article in one sitting. Magazines are sometimes referred to as **periodicals** because they are published during regular periods of time: weekly, monthly, or quarterly.

▶ **Choose a magazine from your school library and fill in the following information.**

1. Name and date of magazine _____

2. Does the magazine have a table of contents? _____
   How is it organized? _____

3. What is the cost of a single copy of this magazine? (Not all magazines are sold individually.) _____

4. How often is the magazine published? _____

5. What is the address of the magazine publisher? _____
   _____

6. Who is the main editor of this magazine? (An editor is the person in charge of writing and publishing the magazine.) _____

7. How many pages is the magazine? _____

8. What is the main topic covered in this magazine? _____

Magazine Contents

<table>
<tr><td>Questions and Answers about the Chinook Tribe .... page 6</td></tr>
<tr><td>   by Ellen Harsog</td></tr>
<tr><td>Struggle for a Homeland—A History .... page 10</td></tr>
<tr><td>   by Kathleen Burk</td></tr>
<tr><td>Cherokee Basket Game and Activity............................... page 15</td></tr>
<tr><td>Sequoia and the Talking Leaves .... page 16</td></tr>
<tr><td>   by Peter Doop</td></tr>
<tr><td>The Trail of Tears—The Cherokee Removal .... page 20</td></tr>
<tr><td>   by Elizabeth Tenny</td></tr>
<tr><td>The Great Chiefs... page 28</td></tr>
<tr><td>   by Elizabeth West</td></tr>
<tr><td>Borrowed Names—Native American Word Game.......... page 31</td></tr>
<tr><td>   by Peg Schabel</td></tr>
</table>

▶ **Use the sample magazine contents above to answer the questions. Remember article names are put in quotation marks.**

1. What article will give you some of the history of the Cherokee tribe?

_____

2. "The Great Chiefs" begins on what page? _____

3. Which article is written by Ellen Harsog? _____

_____

4. If you were interested in doing a craft activity, which article would you read?

_____

5. What is the title of the article on page 16? _____

_____

Using a Magazine Guide

Dinosaurs

"Bones." *Fossil Magazine*. Jan. '01, p. 27–29.

"How the Dinosaur Found Food." *History Magazine*. Sept. '02, p. 21.

"Plants and the Dinosaurs." *Fossil Magazine*. Mar. '02, p. 17.

"Pictures of Prehistoric Dinosaurs." *Art Magazine*. Nov. '04.

"Poems About Dinosaurs." *Poetry Magazine*. June '03, p. 13.

"Songs and Plays About Dinosaurs for Children." *Children's Magazine*. April '02, p. 33.

"The Truth About Dinosaurs." *Dinosaur Magazine*. May '01, p. 3.

"The Truth About Why Dinosaurs Disappeared." *Dinosaur and Reptile Magazine*. June '03, p. 27.

Use the sample magazine guide above to answer the questions.

1. What magazine will give you poems about dinosaurs? _____

   _____

2. You need several pictures for your report about dinosaurs. What magazine will give you the most help? _____

   _____

3. Your younger brother will be in a play about dinosaurs. He plans to sing a song about dinosaurs. What magazine will help him? _____

   _____

4. Why did dinosaurs disappear? What magazine will help? _____

   _____

5. What plants existed during dinosaur times? What magazine will help?

   _____

Name _____ Date _____

Genres of Literature

Genre means a type of writing with characteristics you can recognize. Biographies, science fiction, poetry, and fantasy are all examples of genres.

▶ **Circle the correct answer to identify each genre.**

1. A story set on another planet would probably be—

   science fiction.   **biography.**   **historical fiction.**

2. A book of haiku written in the fifteenth century would be—

   drama.   **poetry.**   **adventure.**

3. A book set in New Orleans during the American Civil War would most likely be—

   fairy tale.   **fantasy.**   **historical fiction.**

4. A book about the life of Martin Luther King, Jr. would be—

   poetry.   **biography.**   **mystery.**

5. A book with talking animals as characters would probably be—

   biography.   **adventure.**   **folktale.**

▶ **Write the genre next to each title.**

6. *Cinderella* _____

7. *Middle School on Mars* _____

8. *The Life of Sitting Bull* _____

9. *The Knight and the Dragon* _____

10. *Rhymes for All Seasons* _____

Poetry

Poetry does not have to be mysterious or difficult to understand. It is simply another way to share thoughts and feelings. Why does a writer write poetry? To tell you something or to show you something.

How do you read a poem? A poem should be read several times.

- First, read the poem from beginning to end without stopping. In this way, you can get an overview of what the poem is about.

- In your second reading, read each line or part of the poem to see if you understand the language. Write down any words you do not understand.

- On your third reading, notice how the poem makes you feel. Each person will have different thoughts and feelings in response to a poem.

It also helps to read the poem out loud. Because poems use words so carefully, speaking the words out loud helps you hear the rhythms and rhymes the poet used.

To help you think about the elements of a poem, answer the questions below about one of your friends.

1. What type of person is your friend (honest, loyal, reliable, sneaky, not to be trusted)? This is called **character**. _____

2. What does your friend look like (tall, short, dark hair, large eyes, small nose)? This is **description**. _____

3. How does your friend sound when talking with you (happy, nervous, angry, sad)? This is called **tone**. _____

4. What does your friend say to you? What are your friend's opinions and feelings about what is being said? This is your friend's **point of view**. _____

_____

Poetry

➡ **Read the poem and answer the questions below.**

I have planted a memory tree,
neither too great
nor too small.
A tree for life,
to celebrate the beauty around me
and to remind me.

May this tree of life I have set to earth
grow roots strongly anchored,
grow branches stretching wide,
to remind me often
of a grandparent's arms
and that loving embrace.

1. Write a summary of the poet's message. _____

_____

_____

2. What does the poet remember? _____

_____

_____

3. What is the poet celebrating? _____

_____

4. Which word is a synonym for *secured*? _____

_____

5. Which words show the poet is joyful? _____

_____

Realistic Fiction

Realistic fiction is a story that could happen, with characters and actions similar to everyday life. You can easily relate to the character's feelings and problems. The story is set in contemporary times, not in a period of history. What makes the story fiction rather than nonfiction is that it is not about a real person or real events.

▶ **Read the passages below. Decide if each passage is realistic fiction or not and circle your choice. Then explain why or why not on the line.**

1. I hopped on the magne-van after my group meeting at the Edu-plex. We had met to discuss our group research, entitled "Foods Across the Galaxies." We could have met by video phone, but our mentor, Sean Wang, suggested that we meet in person.

This passage is: **realistic fiction.**   **not realistic fiction.**

I know because _____ .

2. I want nothing to do with the flower store! I want to work at the art gallery. Mrs. Fleming suggested that I assist her with her Saturday morning class. Those small children are so much fun to teach. But Mom wants me to help her. I just don't know what to do.

This passage is: **realistic fiction.**   **not realistic fiction.**

I know because _____ .

3. Pa handed me the musket. His leg was hurt and I knew it was up to me to help out. "Jesse," he mumbled. "You have to find some game for your ma. Then you can drive the horses so our wagon can rejoin the others. We just have to make it to our homestead out west. I know you can do it, son."

This passage is: **realistic fiction.**   **not realistic fiction.**

I know because _____ .

Name _____ Date _____

Realistic Fiction Sharing Sheet

Title of book _____

Author _____

Copyright date _____   **Number of pages** _____   **Level** _____

1. What is the setting of the story? (Where and when does it take place?)

_____

2. Who is the main character in the story? _____

_____

3. What is the main character's problem in the story? _____

_____

4. How did the main character solve the problem? _____

_____

5. How would you have solved the problem? _____

_____

6. What did you learn from reading this story? _____

_____

7. Could this story really happen? Why or why not? _____

_____

8. Did you like this book? Why or why not? _____

_____

_____

_____

_____

Name _____ Date _____

Science Fiction

Science fiction is a story that is based on a world controlled by scientific development and technology. Many common elements of science fiction stories include predicting the future, living on other planets, alien life, space wars, and futuristic technology.

Science fiction writers love to predict the future. Although many things you read about in science fiction seem impossible, people long ago thought the same thing about spacesuits and television. They did not think these things would ever be invented, but they were! So next time you read a science fiction story, be on the lookout for examples of futuristic technology. The science fiction you are reading may one day become science fact!

► **Design a space city of the future. Include several things that do not exist in our world today. Draw and describe your city in the space below.**

Name of city _____

Where is it located? _____

Futuristic objects in the city _____

Name _____ Date _____

Science Fiction Sharing Sheet

Title of book _____

Author _____

Copyright date _____   **Number of pages** _____   **Level** _____

1. What is the setting of the story? (Where and when does it take place?)

   _____

2. Does this setting seem real? Why or why not? _____

   _____

3. List some things in this book that do not exist in our world today. _____

   _____

4. Who is the most interesting character in the story? Describe the character.

   _____

5. What is the problem in the story? _____

   _____

6. How is the problem solved? _____

   _____

7. Pretend you are a character in this book. Who would you be, and what would

   you like to see happen in the story? _____

   _____

8. Did you like this book? Why or why not? _____

   _____

   _____

   _____

   _____

Folktales

A **folktale** is a story that has been shared orally and passed down for generations. Fairy tales can include many elements of folktales. There are often generic settings and repeated phrases in folktales, such as "once upon a time" or "long ago and far away."

Characters in a folktale represent either good or evil (the bad wolf, the wicked witch, the good prince). Folktales also feature magic and trickery (magic beans, magic numbers, mistaken identities). Action in a folktale is fast-paced and lively. Good is rewarded and evil is punished, making sure that the story ends "happily ever after."

▶ **Ask an adult or a friend to tell you a folktale out loud as he or she remembers it. (Do not read one together.) This is how stories were shared long ago, before there were books. Your job is to write down the name of the tale and the elements of a folktale listed below.**

1. Who are the good characters, and how do you know they are good?

   _____

2. Who are the bad characters, and how do you know they are bad?

   _____

3. What big problem did the main character have to overcome?

   _____

4. What magic or trickery is in the tale? _____

   _____

5. Which do you like best, having a story read to you or told to you out loud? Why?

   _____

   _____

Fractured Folktale

▶ **Choose a folktale. Then fracture it to pieces by filling in the chart below with details about the story.**

setting

good characters

major problem

bad characters

first event

second event

magic or trickery

repeated words or phrases

final event

Tall Tales

Tall tales are American folktales told early in United States history. When the first settlers began moving west, they found themselves faced with seemingly impossible tasks. The huge job of clearing the land to build homes, cities, and railroads gave the workers a chance to invent stories about their surroundings and "larger-than-life" people who felt that nothing was impossible. Some of these legendary heroes were real people. As more people told the stories, they grew, and grew, and grew, until the real live people were no longer human, but fictitious super-beings. For this reason, these stories are called tall tales.

Here are some American tall tale heroes and heroines:

Johnny Appleseed	Paul Bunyan	Joe Magarac
Pecos Bill	Febolb Feboldson	Davy Crockett
Jim Bridger	John Henry	Stormalong
Strap Buckner	Casey Jones	Sally Ann Thunder Ann Whirlwind

Pick three of the characters from the list above. Do some research about the tall tale for each one. Then draw the characters on the map in the location where they gained their fame. Be sure to write the name next to each one.

Tall Tale Activities

Refer to the list of tall tale characters on page 94 to use with the following activities.

1. Pick five to eight tall tale characters and place them on a time line showing each character's beginnings in American history. Tell what was going on in history at the time of each character's story.

2. Think of a "tall tale" that a friend, parent, grandparent, or other relative has told you. Tell the story briefly in a paragraph. Illustrate your tale.

3. Think of a famous person from today's times that would make a good character in a tall tale. Write a modern-day tale about the person you choose.

4. From the list on page 94, choose three characters and research them in the library. For each hero, explain if the character grew from a real person's life story, or if he/she was totally imaginary. Then tell the story of the tall tale in your own words. (You might even want to make the tale even "taller" by adding more exaggeration!)

5. Make a *real* tall tale. Draw scenes from your favorite tall tale on blank sheets of paper. When you are finished, tape the sheets in order from top to bottom to make one long column. Hang your creation high on a wall or ceiling to display your tall tale.

Name _____ Date _____

Web

When you are doing research, a graphic organizer can help you organize your thoughts and the information you find. You can use a **web** to brainstorm a list of possible topics, to connect related ideas in the texts you read, or to help you decide how to order the information you have found. Your main topic goes in the middle circle. Related concepts or ideas go in the surrounding circles.

▶ **Use the blank web below to help with your research.**

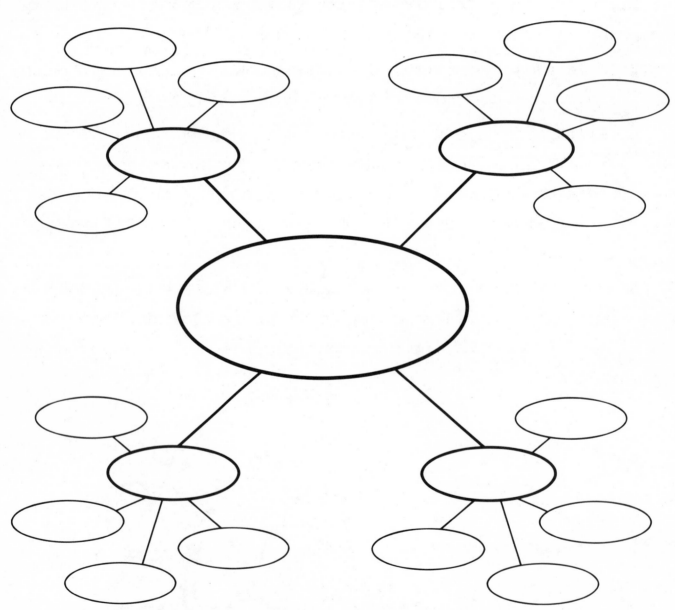

KWL Chart

When you are doing research, a graphic organizer can help you organize your thoughts and the information you find. You can use a **KWL chart** as you begin a research project. This will help you determine the exact areas you need to explore for more information and record what you learn.

▶ **Use the KWL chart below to help with your research.**

What I **KNOW**	What I **WANT** to Know	What I **LEARNED**

Venn Diagram

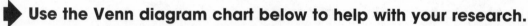

➤ When you are doing research, a graphic organizer can help you organize your thoughts and the information you find. A **Venn diagram** is particularly useful when you are comparing two topics. Record details about the topics in each circle. In the overlapping section, write details that both topics share.

➤ **Use the Venn diagram chart below to help with your research.**

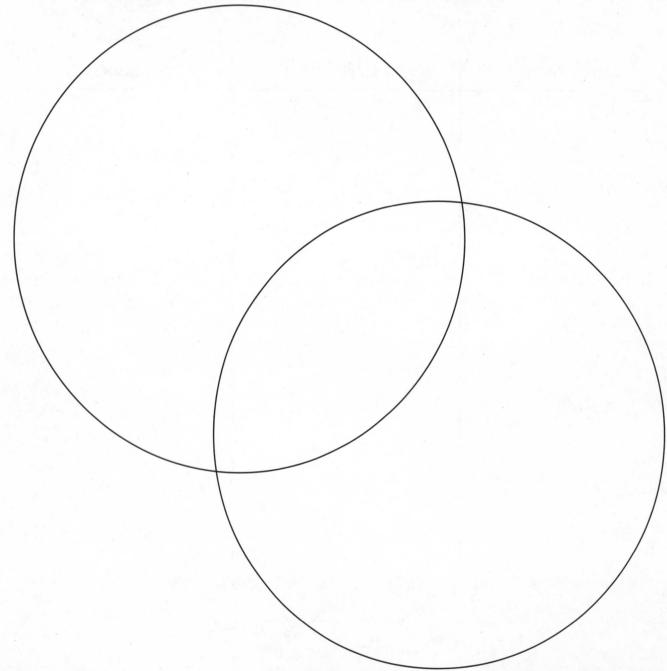

Time Line

▶ When you are doing research, a graphic organizer can help you organize your thoughts and the information you find. You can use a **time line** to record dates in history, in a person's life, steps in a scientific process, or even events in a story.

▶ **Use the time line below to help with your research.**

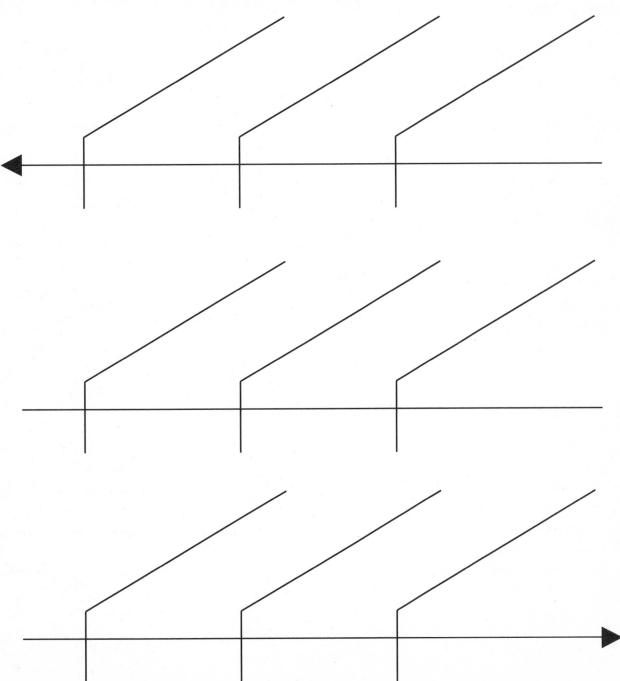

Spider Map

When you are doing research, a graphic organizer can help you organize your thoughts and the information you find. You can use a **spider map** to help you arrange your notes.

▶ **Put the central idea, topic, or theme in the circle. Use the "legs" of the spider to record details.**

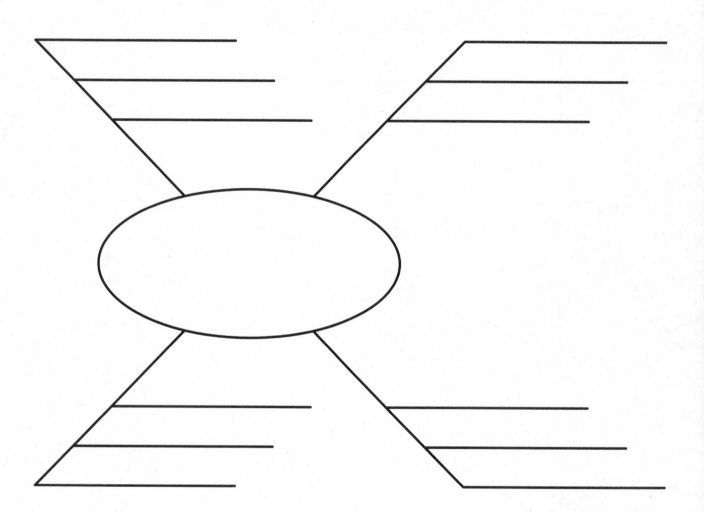

100

Name _____ Date _____

Fishbone

When you are doing research, a graphic organizer can help you organize your thoughts and the information you find. You can use a **fishbone** structure to help you arrange your notes. It is good for showing cause and effect relationships.

▶ **Use the fishbone below to help with your research.**

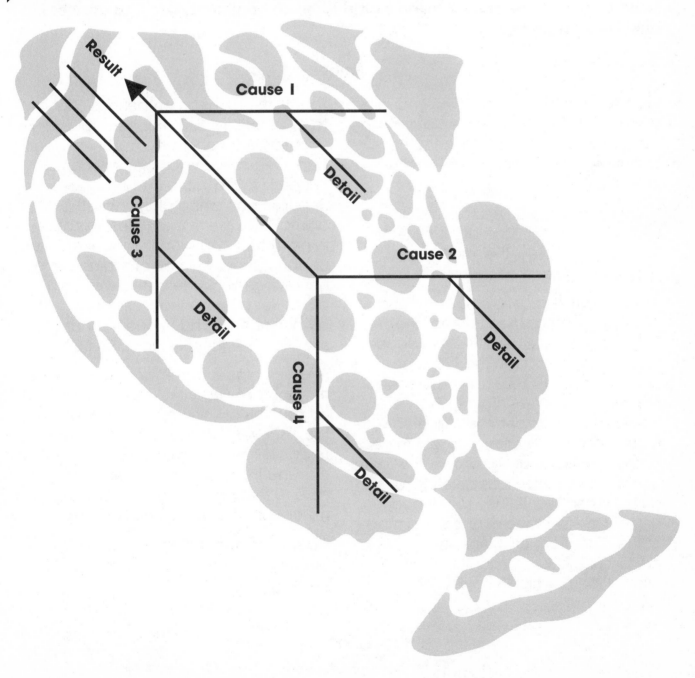

Result

Cause 1

Detail

Cause 2

Detail

Cause 3

Detail

Cause 4

Detail

Fact and Opinion

As you read texts in your library or on the Internet, it is important to be able to recognize the difference between a **fact** (something that is verifiably true) and an **opinion** (what one person thinks about a topic that may or may not be true). You should never state someone's opinion as if it were a fact.

▶ **Read the article below. It contains both facts and opinions. Use it to answer the questions on page 103.**

Amber

Where can you find 100-million-year-old dinosaur blood? From amber, a material known more as a decoration that something of scientific value—that is, until recently.

Amber is hardened tree sap that has become fossilized. Most of it is mined in the Baltic Sea area. It is smooth and warms quickly to the touch.

Amber has been used as a gemstone since pre-historic times. Perhaps the height of amber's beauty could be seen in a Russian palace. In the 1700s, an entire room of 100,000 carved amber pieces was given as a gift to Tsar Peter the Great. This golden room, lighted with more than 500 candles, was said to be dazzling in its beauty. However, the room is now missing. The Nazis stole the room during World War II. They took it apart and hid it. A replacement is being made of the room from drawings and paintings. The search continues for the original room, which is now worth $200 million.

Today, the focus on amber has changed to its scientific value. This gemstone helps scientists learn about life millions of years ago. One in every 100 pieces of amber currently found in the Dominican Republic contains a plant, insect, or tiny animal from prehistoric times. This once-living matter captured in amber can tell us about those animals and plants and how living things interacted with each other. Because of discoveries from amber, scientists have had to change some of their theories about evolution.

An even bigger breakthrough has been the ability to find the DNA of insects in amber. This ability may one day lead to the discovery of dinosaur DNA. How? If a fossilized insect bit a dinosaur, it might be carrying that DNA. The problem is being able to recognize dinosaur DNA from millions of other sequences of DNA.

From art to science, the amazing story of amber continues!

Fact and Opinion (cont.)

Refer to the article on page 102. Write _F_ for fact and _O_ for opinion to identify each sentence below.

1. _____ Amber is hardened tree sap that has been fossilized.

2. _____ Because of amber, scientists have had to change some theories about evolution.

3. _____ DNA research is the most significant scientific breakthrough this planet has ever known.

4. _____ Most amber is mined in the Baltic Sea area.

5. _____ The amber room was the most beautiful work of art from the 1700s.

6. _____ The amber room of Tsar Peter the Great is worth $200 million.

7. _____ The Nazis should not have taken the amber room during World War II.

8. _____ Many pieces of amber contain fossilized insects, plants, or animals.

9. _____ The study of dinosaur DNA is dangerous.

10. _____ Amber is more useful for science than for art.

Paraphrasing

To **quote** means to repeat the exact words that a person said or wrote. It's usually okay to quote someone, as long as you place the words in quotation marks and give credit by writing the person's name at the end of the quote.

You can also use the words someone said or wrote if you rewrite them in your own words. This is called **paraphrasing**. However, you still need to credit the person if you are paraphrasing.

Using someone else's ideas or words without giving credit is called **plagiarism**. That's another word for "copying." To make sure you don't copy by mistake, take short notes in your own words.

Common knowledge is information that can be found in lots of places and includes dates, names, places, and scientific or historical facts.

▶ **Read the sentences. If the sentence is a quote, write Q. If it is a paraphrase, write P. If it is common knowledge, write C.**

1. _____ Principal Kramer said, "We are very proud of the students in this school."

2. _____ Principal Kramer thinks that the students in this school are doing a good job.

3. _____ "When in doubt, wait it out." —General R. J. Wilton

4. _____ Helen Keller was born in 1880.

5. _____ Horace Greeley believed that the American West was a land of opportunity.

6. _____ "Go West, young man, and grow up with the country." —Horace Greely

Paraphrasing Practice

Read the information below. Underline the main idea. Then take notes about this information on the Note Cards shown on page 106. Practice paraphrasing the information you read. Remember, when taking notes, don't copy exactly what is written in the source. Use your own words.

Animal Astronauts

Animals have often led the way for human explorers. The journey into space is no different. The first animals to survive a trip into near space were a monkey and 11 mice on a United States Aerobee sounding rocket in the early 1950s. They rode straight up and then down again.

Russian space dog, Laika, is thought of as the first true space traveler from Earth. *Laika* in Russian means "barker." In 1957, she was the only passenger aboard the Soviet spacecraft *Sputnik 2.* Laika survived for ten days in orbit, but she died before the craft crashed back to Earth.

The first living creatures to survive a controlled ride on an American craft were Able and Baker, a pair of squirrel monkeys. They rode in a capsule atop a *Jupiter C* rocket in 1959. A chimp named Ham is the official holder of the title "first chimpanzee on a U.S. space flight." He made his journey in 1961. He trained for his space flight by learning to pull certain levers when he saw flashing lights. Each time he chose the correct lever, he was rewarded with a banana pellet. After his space capsule landed in the ocean, it almost sank. But Ham was pulled to safety. Another chimp, Enos, was the first American animal to orbit Earth. He made two circuits and returned alive.

Note Cards

Use these note cards as you do your research. Remember to put the title, author, publisher and publishing date, and page number for each quote or fact you record. You can make multiple copies of these cards and cut them apart to help you organize them before you begin writing.

Outlining

An **outline** is a "skeleton" of a story, speech, or report. It is used to organize and put together all your notes.

- **Main ideas (points)** are noted with Roman numerals followed by a period.

- **Subpoints** are indented and are noted with capital letters followed by a period.

- **Supporting details** are indented and noted with numerals followed by a period. **Further details** are noted with lowercase letters followed by a period. There must be at least two details in order to list them.

There are two main styles of traditional outlines:

1. A **topic-only outline** is written in brief simple phrases. There aren't periods after each phrase.

2. A **sentence outline** is written in detailed, complete sentences, which may be used as topic sentences for paragraphs. Words or sentences in equal positions should be of equal importance.

Sample Topic-Only Outlines

Correct:

I. Birds

  A. Pelicans

  B. Penguins

    1. Emperor penguins

    2. King penguins

    3. Macaroni penguins

II. Mammals

  A. Dogs

    1. Golden retrievers

    2. Beagles

  B. Cats

Incorrect:

I. Birds

II. Pelicans

III. Penguins

IV. Emperor penguins

Outlining Practice

An outline is a "skeleton" of a story, speech, or report. It is used to organize and pull together all your notes. See page 107 for more information on outlines.

➡ **Use the following informative article to make an outline for a science report about Venus. Circle the main ideas. Underline the subtopics. Write your outline on page 109.**

Venture to Venus

Venus is the second planet from the sun. It is slightly smaller than Earth, with a diameter of about 7,500 miles.

Volcanic eruptions have covered much of the surface with lava flows. It is a barren planet with huge plains and lowlands. There are two important highland areas, Aphrodite Terra, which is about the size of Africa; and Ishtar Terra, similar in size to Australia. The highest point on Venus is in the Maxwell Montes on Ishtar. It includes a peak that soars seven miles above the surface.

The atmosphere of Venus is made up mostly of carbon dioxide. It acts like a blanket to keep in heat, and the temperatures may reach 900 degrees Fahrenheit—that is hot enough to melt lead! Atmospheric pressure at the surface of the planet is 90 times greater than that of Earth. Venus is covered with a layer of clouds and sulfuric acid, which lead to acid rain, most of which probably evaporates in the extreme heat before it reaches the surface.

Venus spins in the opposite direction of Earth. That means that on Venus, the sun rises in the west and sets in the east. It spins very slowly, taking 243 Earth days to complete one complete turn on its axis. Since Venus completes one orbit around the sun in 225 Earth days, a day on Venus is longer than its year.

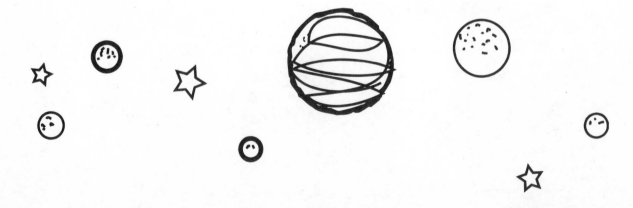

Outlining Practice (cont.)

▶ **Use what you have read on page 108 to create an outline for a science report about Venus. You may not need every line.**

Title _____

   I. Main idea _____

     A. Subtopic _____

       1. Subtopic detail _____

       2. Subtopic detail _____

     B. Subtopic _____

       1. Subtopic detail _____

       2. Subtopic detail _____

  II. Main idea _____

     A. Subtopic _____

       1. Subtopic detail _____

       2. Subtopic detail _____

     B. Subtopic _____

       1. Subtopic detail _____

       2. Subtopic detail _____

 III. Main idea _____

     A. Subtopic _____

       1. Subtopic detail _____

       2. Subtopic detail _____

     B. Subtopic _____

       1. Subtopic detail _____

       2. Subtopic detail _____

Summarizing

▶ **Read the passages below. Pay attention to the details. You will need them to answer the questions on page 111.**

Dolphins

These carnivorous ocean-dwelling mammals live in coastal waters, bays, and lagoons around the world. With keen hearing, they are capable of detecting noises at frequencies up to seven times those detectable by humans. Dolphins harvest fish using their built-in sonar, or echolocation. They make clicking noises underwater and decipher the location of their prey by the returning sound waves that bounce off objects. A group of dolphins is known as a pod. Scientists consider this creature to be among the most intelligent of all animal life.

Baboons

These omnivorous land-loving primates are found in parts of Africa and Arabia. They prefer life on the ground to the tree-climbing life of their cousins, the monkeys. They are easily identified by their long faces, overhanging brows, and their colorful, hairless backsides. They have a good sense of smell and eat small mammals, crustaceans, insects, and other tiny crawling creatures. They also feed on plants and fruit. One baboon species, the gelada, grazes the grasslands for its nourishment. Baboons have large cheek pouches in which they can store their food for easy travel. A group of baboons is called a troop and may range in number from 30 to 100 members.

Squirrels

These primarily herbivorous rodents can be found in all parts of the world except Australia and Antarctica. All but the ground squirrel live in trees. They differ from one another in size. The pygmy squirrel of Africa may stretch to five inches (13 cm) in length, while the giant squirrel of Asia can easily grow to a 36 inch (90 cm) length. They love to eat buds, seeds, and nuts, but often will feast on insects. Squirrels help spread trees and plants throughout the countryside by scattering and storing seeds. Different subfamilies may be red, brown, gray, or blue. The woolly flying squirrel with a body and tail each 2 feet (30 cm) long was thought to be extinct until it was rediscovered in the Himalayan Mountains.

Summarizing (cont.)

▶ **When doing research, it is important to be able to make clear and accurate summaries of what you have read. Practice doing this with the passage on page 110. Match the details below with each of the animals. Cross off the three details that match none of the animals.**

carnivore	echolocation	good sense of smell
flying	herbivore	howler
live in trees	long faces	no tail
ocean-dwelling	omnivore	land-loving
pods	related to cat	rodent
store seeds	troop	very intelligent

Dolphins   **Baboons**   **Squirrels**

_____   _____   _____

_____   _____   _____

_____   _____   _____

_____   _____   _____

_____   _____   _____

▶ **Write a one-sentence summary of the differences between these animals.**

_____

_____

_____

0-7424-1955-X *Complete Library Skills*

Name _____ Date _____

Creating a Bibliography

Book Bibliography

A bibliography is an alphabetized list of resources you used to write your report. It is alphabetized by the writers' last names. Let's say you found some of the information for your report on sailboats in the book *The Story of Boats*. It was written by T. H. Sail in Boatweave, New Jersey, in 2003 by Wave Press Publishers. Your bibliography entry will look like this:

Sail, T. H. *The Story of Boats*. Boatweave, New Jersey: Wave Press, 2003.

Magazine Bibliography

Writing the bibliography for a magazine is much like writing one for a book. First write the author's name (last name first). Then write the name of the article in quotes. Write the name of the magazine in *italics*. Be certain to write its date. Finally, include the page numbers on which the article is found. Let's say that you found information about training parakeets in *Pet Magazine* in an article written by William Rogers called, "How to Train Your Parakeet" (April 7, 1999) on pages 85–87. Your bibliography entry will look like this:

Rogers, William. "How to Train Your Parakeet." *Pet Magazine* (April 7, 1999), 85–87.

Encyclopedia Bibliography

Writing the bibliography for an encyclopedia entry is slightly different from a book. The title of the encyclopedia article comes first in quotes. The title of the encyclopedia follows, and then the year or edition. After the date comes the volume number and the pages for the article. Let's say you find information about pirates in the *Encyclopedia of History* (2001) in an article called "Pirates." Your bibliography entry will look like this:

"Pirates." *Encyclopedia of History*. 2001. Volume 18, pp. 188–191.

Bibliography Practice

Read the information below. Then write it in correct bibliography form. Use the examples on page 112 to help you.

1. Your facts are from an article called "Snakes" by C. Slink in *Science Digest* (June 17, 1999) page 75.

_____

2. *Baseball,* by Roger Base was written in 2001 and published by Diamond Press in Diamond, New York.

_____

3. *Sports Legends,* by Richard Base, was written in 2002 and published by Legend Press in Diamond, New York.

_____

4. Your facts are from an article called "Starting Your Rock Collection" in volume 20 of the *Encyclopedia of Science* (1999) on page 10.

_____

5. Your facts are from an article called "Bicycle Safety" by John Ride in *Hobby Digest* (June 21, 2002) on page 65.

_____

6. *Starfish,* by Linda Sea, was published in 2003 by Wave Press in Oceanside, New Jersey. _____

7. Your facts are from an article called "The Movies" in volume 12 of the *Encyclopedia of Science* (2002) on page 39.

_____

8. Your facts are from an article "Learning to Paint" by C. W. Brush in *Arts and Crafts* (August 8, 2004) on page 65.

_____

Name _____ Date _____

Journaling

➤ **Writing in a journal is a good way to keep track of your responses to literature. After you finish reading a book, take a few minutes right away to put some thoughts in your journal. Then, go back later and answer questions about what you have read. You may use the questions below as a guide for your response. Answer them in a separate notebook or on a sheet of paper.**

Book title _____

Author _____

1. What are your thoughts after finishing this book? Did you enjoy reading it? What were the most memorable things about the book (any words, phrases, events, or scenes that stick with you)?

2. Do any of the characters in the book remind you of people you know? Who? How are they similar?

3. What feelings did the book bring up for you? What events in your own life were you reminded of after reading?

4. Was there anything in the book that confused you (words you didn't know, something you still wonder about, scenes that didn't make sense, scenes that surprised you)?

5. Make a list of your favorite quotes from the book. Use a table similar to the one below to record the quotes and then what your response was after reading it.

Quote (with page number)	My Response

0-7424-1955-X *Complete Library Skills*

Character Map

Use the web below to explore a character in more detail. Put the character's name in the center circle. On the lines coming out, list a trait the character has (such as honesty, bravery, fearfulness, or stubbornness). Then in the box, write an event from the book in which the character demonstrates that trait.

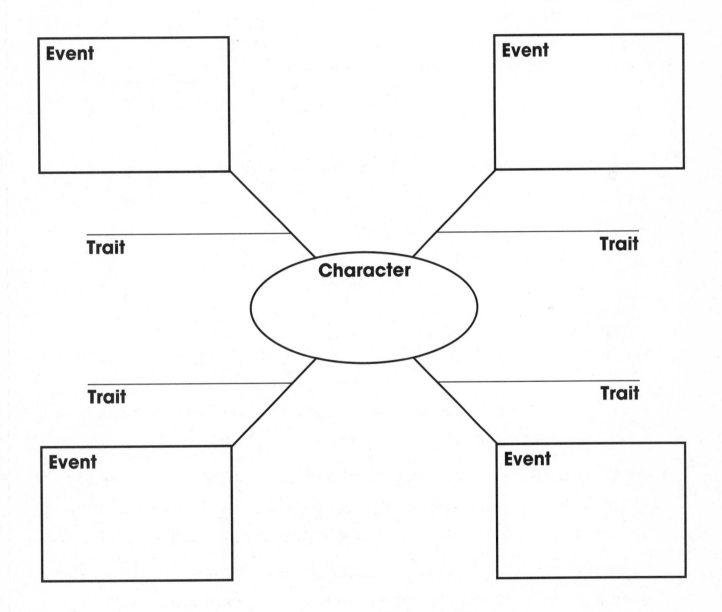

Event

Event

Trait

Trait

Character

Trait

Trait

Event

Event

0-7424-1955-X *Complete Library Skills*

Tips for Writing a Book Report

Writing a book report is a good way of showing your teacher that you have read and understood the book you chose. It can also inform your friends and classmates about a book they should (or shouldn't!) read.

Here are some tips for writing a book report.

1. First, state the title, author, and the year the book was published. (If the book has pictures, name the illustrator as well.)

2. Next, state why you think the book is worthwhile or not worthwhile. Be careful not to use words like "good," "great," or "interesting." Try using descriptive words like those listed below.

funny	biographical	sad	inspiring
scary	historical	suspenseful	amusing
lifelike	imaginary	romantic	scientific

3. After talking about your book in a general sense, write a little about the most exciting part of the book—but don't tell everything! Remember, if you liked the book, you want to get others to read it. If you tell about all of the exciting parts, no one will need to read it.

4. As you write your report, be careful that you don't just retell the story. Tell a little about an exciting part to get your audience interested, but remember that your primary goal should be telling why people should (or should not) read the book.

5. At the end of your report, write a short paragraph on the author (and/or illustrator). This will let your audience know something about the author's background and how this may have been a basis for the story or the author's style of writing.

Name _____ Date _____

Make a Book Report Commercial

➤ **Pretend that you are a salesperson whose job it is to sell your favorite book. Write a commercial to persuade listeners to read the book. Use the suggestions below to help you get started. Remember, you don't want to retell the story, just inspire people to read it.**

Some things to include in your commercial:

- title of the book

- author

- details from the author's life if they are relevant to the story

- genre of the book (e.g., mystery, historical fiction, realistic fiction, science fiction)

- how the book is different from others; what makes it unique

- what the main character is like

- a "cliffhanger" from the story (describe part of an exciting event but not how it turns out)

_____

_____

_____

_____

_____

_____

_____

_____

_____

_____

_____

Suggested Titles for Fifth-Grade Readers

Newbery Award Winners

2003—*Crispin: The Cross of Lead* by Avi

2002—*A Single Shard* by Linda Sue Park

2001—*A Year Down Yonder* by Richard Peck

2000—*Bud, Not Buddy* by Christopher Paul Curtis

1999—*Holes* by Louis Sachar

1998—*Out of the Dust* by Karen Hesse

1997—*The View from Saturday* by E. L. Konigsburg

1996—*The Midwife's Apprentice* by Karen Cushman

1995—*Walk Two Moons* by Sharon Creech

Coretta Scott King Award Winners

2003—*Bronx Masquerade* by Nikki Grimes

2002—*The Land* by Mildred Taylor

2001—*Miracle's Boys* by Jacqueline Woodson

2000—*Bud, Not Buddy* by Christopher Paul Curtis

1999—*Heaven* by Angela Johnson

1998—*Forged by Fire* by Sharon M. Draper

1997—*Slam!* by Walter Dean Myers

Nonfiction

Barr, George. *Sports Science for Young People.*

Conlan, K. E. *Under the Ice.*

Fleischman, John. *Phineas Gage: A Gruesome But True Story About Brain Science.*

Frank, Anne. *Anne Frank, The Diary of a Young Girl.*

Hoose, Phillip. *It's Our World Too: Stories of Young People Who Are Making a Difference.*

Jackson, D. *Bone Detectives.*

Lawrence, R. D. *Wolves.*

Macaulay, David. *The Way Things Work.*

Muñoz Ryan, Pam. *When Marian Sang: The True Recital of Marian Anderson—The Voice of a Century.*

O'Connor, Jane. *The Emperor's Silent Army: Terracotta Warriors of Ancient China.*

Old, Wendy C. *To Fly: The Story of the Wright Brothers.*

Simon, S. *Comets, Meteors, and Asteroids.*

Biography

Freedman, Russel. *Lincoln: A Photobiography.*

Fritz, Jean. *And Then What Happened, Paul Revere?*

Hargrove, Jim. *Steven Spielberg: Amazing Filmmaker.*

Hickman, Homer H. *Rocket Boys: A Memoir.*

McKissack, Fred and Patricia. *Sojourner Truth: A Voice for Freedom.*

Folktales

Goble, Paul. *The Gift of the Sacred Dog.*

MacDonald, Margaret Read. *Earth Care: World Folktales to Talk About.*

San Souci, R. *Samurai's Daughter.*

Wisniewski, David. *Golem.*

Realistic Fiction

Bauer, Joan. *Sticks.*

Byars, Betsy. *Summer of the Swans.*

Cleary, Beverly. *Dear Mr. Henshaw.*

Clements, Andrew. *Frindle.*

Creech, Sharon. *Love That Dog.*

DeClements, Barthe. *Nothing's Fair in the Fifth Grade.*

Lowry, Lois. *Anastasia Krupnik.*

Simont, Mark. *The Stray Dog.*

Paterson, Katherine. *The Great Gilly Hopkins.*

Paulsen, Gary. *Hatchet.*

Taylor, Mildred D. *Roll of Thunder, Hear My Cry.*

Historical Fiction

Erdrich, Louise. *The Birchbark House.*

Forbes, Esther. *Johnny Tremain.*

Ho, Minfong. *The Clay Marble.*

O'Dell, Scott. *Sing Down the Moon.*

Wilder, Laura Ingalls. *Little House on the Prairie.*

Science Fiction/Fantasy

Alexander, Lloyd. *The Book of Three.*

Babbitt, Natalie. *Tuck Everlasting.*

Christopher, John. *When the Tripods Came.*

Cooper, Susan. *The Dark Is Rising.*

Horvath, Polly. *Everything on a Waffle.*

L'Engle, Madeleine. *A Wrinkle in Time.*

Norton, Mary. *The Borrowers.*

Snicket, Lemony. *A Series of Unfortunate Events.*

Poetry

Clinton, Catherine. *I, Too, Sing America: Three Centuries of African American Poetry.*

Kennedy, X. J. and Dorothy. *Knock at a Star: A Child's Introduction to Poetry.*

Prelutsky, Jack. *The Random House Book of Poetry for Children.*

Silverstein, Shel. *Where the Sidewalk Ends.*

Reading Log

Name _____

Grade _____ **Teacher's Name** _____

Date	Book Title	Author	Genre	Pages

Total Books Read _____

Total Number of Pages Read _____

Total Number of Genres Read _____

Library Superstar

To _____

For _____

This award is proudly presented
in recognition of excellence
using the library and its resources.

Signed _____

Date _____

0-7424-1955-X Complete Library Skills

Glossary of Library Terms

almanac—a book published every year that contains up-to-date facts, charts, and tables about science, history, news and world events, sports, entertainment, and more

appendix—found at the back of the book, an appendix contains information the author wishes to add, such as tables or lists of information

atlas—a bound collection of maps

bibliography—an alphabetized list that tells the sources that were used in a report and includes author's name, title, place and date of publication, and publisher

browser station—a computer station where you can search the library's holdings

card catalog—a collection of cards arranged alphabetically by author, title, or subject

copyright page—found at the front of the book; gives the title, author, publisher, place of publication, and copyright date

dictionary—a book with an alphabetized list of words that shows meaning and pronunciation

encyclopedia—a collection of several volumes (or a searchable reference on a computer) that contains information on people, places, and ideas

genre—a category of literature characterized by a certain style, form, or content

glossary—a "mini-dictionary" that lists in alphabetical order all the important terms presented in the book

graphic organizer—a tool to help organize information by putting it in charts, circles, or other visual layouts

guide letters—letters placed on the top of a page, the spine of a book (encyclopedia), the outside of card catalog drawers, or the library shelves to tell the range of materials found there

Glossary of Library Terms (cont.)

guide words—words at the top of a page (usually in a reference tool) to show the first and last words on the page

heading—a title usually in bold type that summarizes the text below it; found throughout an article, chapter, or entry

index—an alphabetized list of specific topics that can be found in a book

Internet—a network that connects computers all over the world

keyword—one of the main words from a title or document that can be used to search for content

media center—a term to describe libraries and the various media they might contain (books, DVDs, videos, computers)

paraphrase—to restate something using different words than the original source

preface—important facts or thoughts that the author wants you to know; found at the beginning of a book

search engine—computer software created to search a large collection of data for specific information

search terms—the words or phrases used to perform a search; can consist of several keywords together

"see also" references—additional subjects under which you might find information; found at the end of an article or search

skim—to look quickly over a text to determine the main points

table of contents—listing of chapter titles; found at the beginning of a book

thesaurus—a book that lists synonyms (words with similar meanings)

Answer Key

Where to Find It

  1. e
  2. f
  3. g
  4. h
  5. i
  6. j
  7. a
  8. c
  9. b
  10. d

Answers will vary.

  1. subject
  2. title
  3. author
  4. subject

  1. *The Mystery of the Green Parrot*
  2. Sally Feather
  3. Pellet Press in Trenton, New Jersey
  4. Fic Fe
  5. fiction
  6. yes; illus. stands for illustrated

  1. *Caring for Your Pet Parrot*
  2. Polly Pendleton
  3. Birdbrain Publications in Austin, Texas
  4. 636.68 Pe
  5. nonfiction
  6. yes; illus. stands for illustrated

  1. *The Well-Behaved Parrot*
  2. Stuart Cracker
  3. Pet Publications in Los Angeles, California
  4. 636 Cr
  5. nonfiction
  6. yes; illus. stands for illustrated

  1. Yes. A poster might show one of Van Gogh's famous paintings and would be a nice visual aid for your speech.
  2. search under subject "sports"; blue label
  3. search under title; blue label
  4. search under title; yellow or green label

  1. subject
  2. author
  3. title
  4. subject
  5. subject
  6. title
  7. subject
  8. title
  9. author
  10. author

  1. subject
  2. author
  3. subject
  4. title
  5. subject
  6. author
  7. subject
  8. subject
  9. title
  10. author

Answers will vary.

  1. Talia did not need to include the word "the" in her search.
  2. It usually does not matter if you use capital letters when searching.
  3. record 3
  4. a videocassette

  1. 2004
  2. 599 Nu
  3. 111 pages
  4. Tree Press, New Jersey
  5. Yes; summary states that illustrations describe squirrel homes.

  1. squirrel control
  2. squirrels
  3. *Outwitting Squirrels*

Answers may vary.
  1. general; "wildlife" is a broad term
  2. general; all over the world is a large area to cover
  3. specific; names specific animal
  4. specific; narrows topic to just effects on environment
  5. general; could be a huge question to answer

Answers may vary.
  1. solar system planets; space
  2. ladybug; insects
  3. baseball; sports
  4. guinea pig; pets

  1. subject search
  2. narrowed the results
  3. results would not have had to do with training
  4. A keyword search would be more helpful if you wanted to see a broad selection of materials on a topic. A subject search might be more helpful if you wanted more specific results.

Answers may vary.
  1. acid rain **or** rain forest **and** problems
  2. pizza **and** recipes **and not** restaurant
  3. dog **and** grooming **and not** short-haired
  4. CD players **and** portable **or** battery-operated

Answers may vary.
  1. sports stars; sports **and** stars **and** problems
  2. vacation, packing; vacation **and** packing **and** tips
  3. vitamins, nutrition; vitamins **and** nutrition
  4. newspapers, history; newspapers **and** history **and** interpretation
  5. pet care; pets **and** care **or** feeding
  6. weather patterns, world, local; weather patterns **and** world **and** local effects

  1. d
  2. e
  3. a
  4. b
  5. c

Extended Searches..........................25

Answers may vary.

1. headphones, innovations, product information, analyze, evaluation, usage
2. portable stereos, CD players, design and construction, product introduction
3. headphones, equipment and supplies, purchasing, product information
4. headphones, health aspects, safety and security measures
5. portable stereos, CD players, equipment and supplies

Internet Searches 26–27

Answers will vary.

Evaluating Web Sites as Sources 29

1. b; the ".org" indicates a reliable source
2. site a
3. Answers will vary.

Can You Spy the Best Site?.........30–31

1. a; ".edu" indicates an education-related site, National Zoo a well-known organization
2. c; ".gov" indicates a government sponsored site
3. a; ".org" indicates a reliable source
4. b; ".org" indicates a reliable source, ALA is a well-known organization (American Library Association)

Dewey Decimal Classification®.......33

1. 600–699, Medicine and Technology
2. 700–799, Arts and Recreation
3. 400–499, Languages and Grammar
4. 300–399, Social Sciences and Folklore
5. 700–799, Arts and Recreation
6. 800–899, Literature
7. 900–999, Geography and History
8. 000–099, General Works
9. 500–599, Math and Science
10. 100–199, Philosophy and Psychology

Number, Please 34

1. 900–999, Geography and History
2. 200–299, Religion and Mythology
3. 300–399, Social Sciences and Folklore (or 800–899, Literature)
4. 700–799, Arts and Recreation
5. 700–799, Arts and Recreation
6. 600–699, Medicine and Technology
7. 500–599, Math and Science
8. 900–999, Geography and History

Take Two Categories........................35

Answers may vary.

1. Geography and History; Medicine and Technology
2. Literature, Arts and Recreation
3. Geography and History, Medicine and Technology
4. Geography and History, General Works
5. Social Sciences and Folklore, Languages and Grammar
6. Medicine and Technology, Social Sciences and Folklore
7. Geography and History, Math and Science
8. Social Sciences and Folklore, Literature, Geography and History

Dewey Breakdown, Part 1 36

1. 720
2. 790
3. 780
4. 730
5. 750
6. 790
7. 710
8. 770
9. 740
10. 740

Dewey Breakdown, Part 2 37

1. 598
2. 595
3. 596
4. 590 and/or 591
5. 599
6. 599
7. 592 and/or 594
8. 593
9. 597
10. 594

Dewey Breakdown, Part 3 38

1. List 1 correct order: a, e, d, f, b, c
2. List 2 correct order: d, f, a, b, c, e

Dewey Quiz 39

1. 900–999, Geography and History
2. 500–599, Math and Science
3. 400–499, Languages and Grammar
4. 500–599, Math and Science
5. 300–399, Social Sciences and Folklore
6. 700–799, Arts and Recreation
7. 300–399, Social Sciences and Folklore
8. 201.5 Br, 345.1 Ta, 401.5 Tr, 790.1 Br, 791.1 Ba

Reference Materials 40

1. encyclopedia
2. dictionary
3. atlas
4. almanac
5. encyclopedia
6. almanac

Using an Almanac............................41

Answers will vary.

Going to Extremes 42

1. blue whale
2. Kuala Lumpur
3. Mercury
4. China
5. Japan
6. ear
7. California
8. almanac

Know-It-All-Manac............................43

Answers will vary.

Using an Atlas..................................44

1. H-3
2. J-4
3. I-2
4. H-3
5. H-1
6. I-4
7. I-3
8. K-3 (or K-4)

That's Just Capital............................45

1. g
2. e
3. h
4. i
5. b
6. a
7. c
8. j
9. d
10. f

Answer Key

1. Western Australia, Northern Territory, South Australia, Queensland, New South Wales, Victoria, Australian Capital Territory, Tasmania
2. They are all near the coast.
3. sheep and cattle grazing
4. 3 time zones (Eastern Standard Time, Central Standard Time, Western Standard Time)
5. arid, desert
6. Indian Ocean, South Pacific Ocean
7. northeast
8. Tasmania

ace–answer
- action
- after
- always
- animal

ant–auto
- anteater
- apple
- arch
- attention

1. Pitcher, Vol. 17
2. New, Vol. 16
3. Mount, Vol. 14
4. Native, Vol. 15
5. Polo, Vol. 17
6. Monroe, Vol. 14

1. no
2. D:70, T:410
3. B:675, F:74
4. yes, entry for plant leaves
5. yes; V:310 (vegetables)

1. *World of Science Encyclopedia*, G:334–339
2. *Science Times Encyclopedia*, D 125–126
3. *World of Science Encyclopedia*, F:37
4. *Science Times Encyclopedia*, P 107
5. *Science Times Encyclopedia*, D 117–120 (also D 121–123)
6. *World of Science Encyclopedia*, P:111
7. *Science Times Encyclopedia*, D 121–123
8. *World of Science Encyclopedia*, F:138

Answers may vary.
1. e
2. e
3. b, d, e
4. b, d
5. b
6. b
7. b, d
8. e
9. b, c
10. e

Answers may vary.
1. h, j
2. k
3. b, c
4. o
5. i
6. m
7. p
8. c
9. l
10. c

1. space travel; Armstrong, Neal; Glenn, John
2. Halley's Comet
3. wildlife; zoos
4. cider
5. automobile models
6. Wright Brothers; test pilots
7. antennae; any 3 of the following: ant; bee; insect; beetle; butterfly

Answers may vary.
1. *Science Encyclopedia of Today*
2. *American Encyclopedia of History*
3. *The Encyclopedia of Inventions* (or *American Encyclopedia of History*)
4. *Art Today Encyclopedia*
5. *The Encyclopedia of Hobbies* (or *The Collectibles Encyclopedia*)
6. *Science Encyclopedia of Today*
7. *Art Today Encyclopedia*
8. *American Encyclopedia of History*

Answers may vary.
1. *Encyclopedia of World History*
2. *Art in America, Encyclopedia of World History*
3. *Encyclopedia of Inventions, Encyclopedia of Science*
4. *Encyclopedia of World History*

5. *Encyclopedia of Sports*
6. *Encyclopedia of Inventions*
7. *Space and Star Encyclopedia, Encyclopedia of Science*
8. *Encyclopedia of World History*
9. *Hobby Master Encyclopedia*
10. *Hobby Master Encyclopedia, The Collectibles Encyclopedia*

1. bison–blackbird (blackberry)
2. city–crash (coconut)
3. canopy–chirp (cherry)
4. chisel–choir (chocolate)
5. baffle–barge (banana)

1. verb
2. adjective
3. adjective
4. verb
5. verb
6. noun
7. adjective
8. adjective

Word	1	2	3	4
watermelon	█	█	█	█
breakfast	█	█		
servant	█	█		
buffalo	█	█	█	
arch	█			
aggressive	█	█	█	
victim	█	█		
column	█	█		
history	█	█	█	
selection	█	█	█	
margin	█	█		
deception	█	█	█	
pilot	█	█		
compulsory	█	█	█	█
cucumber	█	█	█	
leisure	█	█		
sketch	█			
traditional	█	█	█	█
conventional	█	█	█	█

Number of Syllables

1. five
2. two
3. seven
4. verb, 2: to shut off from view
5. noun, 5: a line of houses enclosed by streets
6. Answers will vary.
7. Answers will vary.

Phonetic Spelling **64**

From inside caves and beneath bridges, these flying creatures come out. Appearing at night, they look for food, dipping and diving about. They see with their ears and not their eyes. Do you know the mammal in this disguise?

This animal is a bat.

The Biographical Dictionary **65**
1. Scotland
2. 1940
3. physician
4. Sir George Buchanan
5. You could look in an encyclopedia for further information. Possible subjects to search include medicine, sanitary science, diseases.

Using the Biographical Dictionary ... **66**
1. *Don Quixote*
2. 1821
3. journalist
4. admiral, explorer
5. 1483
6. "Battle Hymn of the Republic"
7. inventor, educator, botanist
8. Italian
9. American social worker and reformer; established "Hull House"
10. 1452
11. 1913
12. Japanese

Using a Thesaurus **67**
Answers will vary.

What's Inside

Parts of a Book **68**
1. d
2. e
3. a
4. b
5. c

Copyright Page **69**
1. F
2. T
3. T
4. F
5. T

Using the Title and Copyright Pages **71**
1. 1999
2. Sandals, California
3. *Today's Trends in Footwear*, newer and also nonfiction
4. *The Case of the Purple Shoes*; illustrated
5. yes—have city and zip code; possibly no—need street address
6. illustrator of *The Case of the Purple Shoes*
7. *Today's Trends in Footwear*
8. no; only discusses recent trends not history

Table of Contents **72**
1. Book A; two whole chapters on colonies
2. no—doesn't have a chapter on colonies; possibly yes—after checking index
3. no; not enough information about what's inside

Using the Table of Contents **73**
1. page 61
2. page 78
3. page 22
4. page 89
5. page 45
6. page 4

Index **74**
1. yes; four pages
2. no; only has two pages on competitions—not enough for a whole report
3. two pages

The Index Page **75**
1. pages 20–21, 25
2. page 19
3. yes; pages 24–26
4. no
5. yes; page 23
6. avalanche rescue dogs, guide dogs, rescue dogs
7. breeds of dogs, illustrated (pages 24–25)
8. beauty parlors for dogs (page 31)

Using a Book Index **76**
1. ants, places found throughout the world (pages 117–123)
2. ants, red (page 3); ants, brown (pages 17, 39)
3. ants, homes (pages 39–42)

4. ants, food (pages 5, 6, 7)
5. ants, their helpfulness to people (pages 89–94)
6. ants, and termites (page 87)

Using a Book Index **77**
1. pages 7, 15
2. page 17
3. page 27
4. page 13
5. page 5
6. page 17
7. pages 19, 23
8. page 31

Comparing Contents and Index Pages **79**
1. index; pages 12, 34
2. table of contents
3. index; page 14
4. index; pages 8, 20, 21
5. table of contents
6. index; pages 8, 25
7. index; pages 14–16
8. index; page 11

Glossary **80**
1. walking more than one step while holding the ball
2. wouldn't have many chances to make baskets
3. before; in alphabetical order

Using the Glossary **81**
1. Search terms may be made of several keywords.
2. preface—beginning; appendix—end
3. A glossary gives definitions; an index has page numbers.
4. index
5. A heading appears throughout an article, while a "see also" reference appears at the end of the article.
6. author's name, title, place and date of publication, and publisher
7. A card catalog has drawers with cards inside about the library's holdings; a browser station is a computer that can be used to search the library's holdings.
8. Guide letters show you the range of words or books you would find within a page, volume, or shelf.

Magazines **82**
Answers will vary.

Answer Key

Magazine Contents 83
1. "The Trail of Tears—The Cherokee Removal"
2. page 28
3. "Questions and Answers about the Chinook Tribe"
4. "Cherokee Basket Game and Activity"
5. "Sequoia and the Talking Leaves"

Using a Magazine Guide 84
1. *Poetry Magazine*
2. *Art Magazine*
3. *Children's Magazine*
4. *Dinosaur and Reptile Magazine*
5. *Fossil Magazine*

Genres of Literature 85
1. science fiction
2. poetry
3. historical fiction
4. biography
5. folktale
6. fairy tale
7. science fiction
8. biography
9. fantasy
10. poetry

Poetry 86
Answers will vary.

Poetry 87
1. The poet plants a tree to celebrate beauty and remind her of a grandparent who has died.
2. The poet remembers the loving embrace of her grandparent.
3. The poet is celebrating the beauty around her.
4. anchored
5. life, celebrate

Realistic Fiction................................88
1. not realistic fiction; futuristic details not possible in today's world
2. realistic fiction; story in today's world, character's problems
3. not realistic fiction; historical details, set in past

Genre Activities..........................89–95
Answers will vary.

How to Use It

Graphic Organizers 96–101
Answers will vary.

Fact and Opinion............................103
1. F
2. F
3. O
4. F
5. O
6. F
7. O
8. F
9. O
10. O

Paraphrasing 104
1. Q
2. P
3. Q
4. C
5. P
6. Q

Paraphrasing Practice....................105
Answers will vary.

Outlining Practice...........................109
Answers will vary.

Summarizing 111
Dolphins
carnivore
echolocation
ocean-dwelling
pods
very intelligent

Baboons
good sense of smell
long faces
omnivore
land-loving
troop

Squirrels
flying
herbivore
live in trees
store seeds
rodent

No matches for: related to cat, howler, no tail.

Summaries will vary.

Bibliography Practice....................113
1. Slink, C. "Snakes." *Science Digest* (June 17, 1999), 75.
2. Base, Roger. *Baseball*. Diamond, New York: Diamond Press, 2001.
3. Base, Richard. *Sports Legends*. Diamond, New York: Legend Press, 2002.
4. "Starting Your Rock Collection." *Encyclopedia of Science*. 1999. Volume 20, p. 10.
5. Ride, John. "Bicycle Safety." *Hobby Digest* (June 21, 2002), 65.
6. Sea, Linda. *Starfish*. Oceanside, New Jersey: Wave Press, 2003.
7. "The Movies." *Encyclopedia of Science*. 2002. Volume 12, p. 39.
8. Brush, C. W. "Learning to Paint." *Arts and Crafts*. (August 8, 2004), 65.

Literature Activities 114–117
Answers will vary.